NEVER A HO-HUM DAY

STORIES ABOUT A KENTUCKY HILL COUNTRY VETERINARIAN AND HIS 'DOCTORIN'

JOHN G. MARTIN, DVM

Guild Press of Indiana, Inc.
Carmel, IN

By The Same Author

Doc, My Tiger's Got An Itch, Guild Press of Indiana, 1996

It Began At Imphal, Sunflower University Press, 1987

Though Hells Gate to Shanghai, Lawhead Press, 1983

Guild Press of Indiana, Inc.
435 Gradle Drive
Carmel, Indiana 46032

Printed in the United States of America

Library of Congress Catalog Card Number 97-78018

ISBN 1-57860-052-9

To Mary Helen and Terri

CONTENTS

ABOUT MY STORY

NEVER A HO-HUM DAY is based on my career of nearly half a century as a veterinarian in the hill country of eastern Kentucky. It has been a rewarding time and, if asked to do it again, I would do it, ". . . in a heartbeat." Countless numbers of friends and acquaintances have often asked me to tell my stories and so I have. Not every happening was a happy one; some were sad and even tragic. Other stories are funny and reveal the humor of the occasion. The main thing is—all are true. But the story is not really so much about me, even though I was involved in every one of these adventures. It is about eastern Kentucky—the foothills of Appalachia, the people that live here and the happenings of our times. So let me tell you first about our land and then about some of its people.

The countryside is inspiring. It is a land of contrast with rolling hills, deep valleys and lazy, winding rivers. Farther south is the big hill country with deep hollows and rushing mountain streams. The landscape is accentuated with a sprinkling of large and small farms, some nesting in cleared places in the woodlands, others in the hollows and on the hillsides. Beneath the surface is the coal, natural gas and oil that generate energy for its industries. Many small towns and villages dot the area, most started by the pioneers who explored and settled this land many years ago. Most of these places are steeped in history and are now monuments to those early residents of the hills.

In eastern Kentucky we enjoy four distinct seasons, each creating its own scenario. Spring's magic is terrific—white dogwood blossoms and the pink blooms of the redbud trees splash the hillsides with color as the warm sun brings the sleeping, winter hillsides back to life. Then comes the summer season with hot, lazy days and enough rain to grow good tobacco and corn. As the year gets older, the days get shorter and autumn comes in all of its glory, at times nearly taking your breath away, coloring the woods with freshly painted red, brown and yellow leaves. Winters as a rule are not too cold, and when the snow comes it lasts only a short time, the warm sun melting the snow cover and helping it find its way as water trickling down the hollows to the streams and rivers. Eastern Kentucky is a lovely piece of America.

Here in our land live wonderful people. They are mostly plain, hard workers, tending farms or working in the steel mills or factories. Many earn their pay on the railroad, in the coal mines or in their professions. All support strong convictions about their lives, their community and their belief in God.

This is the story about these people and their land. It is about some of the things that happen in a career like mine tending animals—and people in a different way—in a place like this. I would like to share with my readers some of these little adventures that happened to me and my friends during my many years caring for the livestock and pets in the Kentucky hills.

In most cases I have used the real names of the people mentioned, trying in some way to show them my gratitude for being part of my career and my life. In a few cases the names have been changed, for obvious reasons. In no way at all do I cast unkindly remarks or attempt to belittle these people as to how, or where, they live. I simply want to tell my story as I saw it and hopefully can entertain you with some of these adventures.

John G. Martin, DVM

SEEDS

S UNDAY, MARCH 10, 1940, WAS A GUSTY, CHILLY, TYPICAL EARLY SPRING-like day. The sun was shining and the blue sky was a good sign winter had gasped its last. A handful of local horse owners gathered at the Selby horse barn, a boarding and training stable, socializing, grooming and riding their animals, enjoying the long awaited seasonal change.

The telephone in the office rang. No one gave it much thought. Pete, one of the stable employees, was pitch-forking dirty, wet, manure-filled stall bedding into a wheelbarrow, getting ready to replace it with clean, fresh straw. Pete wasn't very enthusiastic about his job and when the phone rang, he quickly put down his pitch fork and went into the office and answered it. The serenity of the morning was shattered when he came out of the stable office, face an ashen white, yelling at the top of his voice, "R.L. Black's horse barn is on fire!" Gasping to get another breath he said, "That was Sally on the phone and she called to tell me about the fire. She said she understood a lot of horses were burned up and maybe some people hurt too!"

Pete was a young fellow who helped with the horses after school and on weekends. Sally was Pete's cousin. She was also the telephone operator in Lucasville, the village just one mile south of the county fairgrounds and ten miles north of my home town, Portsmouth, Ohio. R.L. Black was a horse trader, and besides buying and selling horses, he also boarded and trained horses for other people. He was a shrewd businessman and some jokingly said, "You better watch out when you deal with R.L. He is a slick trader." But in spite of the little jokes, R.L. Black was liked by everyone. After the shock of the phone call wore off and Pete finally regained some of his composure, he said Sally had called him as soon as she reported the fire to the

Lucasville Fire Department. Everybody was stunned by the news, almost in shock. Someone said, as if it was imperative, "Let's go to the fairgrounds."

My father was with me that morning and without any hesitation he said, "Let's go, my car is parked out back!" Several of us ran to his car and we were on our way, trying to fathom the horror of a barn fire and what might have caused it. Father drove as fast as he dared and before we were half way to Lucasville, we could see the billowing, black smoke clouding the clear, blue sky. In just fifteen minutes we turned in through the main gate of the fair-grounds.

The shock of the news on the telephone was terrible, but nothing compared to what we saw. Two of the big barns were on fire. Firemen and their pumper trucks were busy with their hoses, pouring water onto the leaping flames. By this time nearly a hundred people had gathered and watched and helped when they could. Most were kept from the blaze by the intense heat and thick black smoke, but some were leading horses away from the burning buildings to the fenced-off field inside the race track fifty yards away. Others stood in silent groups, many with tears streaming down their faces, and watched helplessly as the suffering animals were led away. Most of these were tied to the fences only to break away and run back into the inferno and certain death. Many of these horses were badly burned, their flesh hanging in horrible, ugly strips from their bodies. Most all of the animals were cough-ing, their lungs destroyed as well as their torsos. By mid afternoon the fire-fighters managed to put out most of the fire, but not until both structures had burned to the ground. Just a few rafters still stood supporting what was left of one burned out roof. Finally, as with a vengeance, they too caved in—both barns now completely destroyed—a smoldering pile of ashes and dead animals.

The fire fighters put away their hoses and only after the smoke died away and the battle was over, did the shock of what had happened become so obvious. Dead horses, most burned beyond recognition as animals, laid in rows, one after another where they burned to death trapped in their stalls with no chance to escape. The odor of burning flesh and charred wood was overpowering. Finally, late in the afternoon when the fire was out, the crowd dispersed and silently moved away. A few looked back as they left, still find-ing it hard to believe what had happened. All together twenty-one fine saddle horses and ponies perished. Of those few survivors most had lasting scars and respiratory trouble. A very few horses escaped without injury. Most of the severely burned ones were later destroyed by the kindness of euthanasia by Dr. Owen Karr, the local veterinarian. Mr. Black, one of his employees, and two horse owners were also burned trying to save their animal's lives.

The fair board eventually had the barns rebuilt with the aid of funds from the WPA. R.L. Black went back into business trading and training horses. The cause of that horrible fire was never determined but it was believed sparks from a passing freight train started it. The railroad tracks were not seventy five feet from the stable. As a young horse lover, this was the very first exposure I had to animal suffering and death.

Horses have fascinated me from the time I first saw one. My very first equine recollection was when I was four or five years old. I had wandered away from our house, much to my mother's concern, up to Gallia Street, one of the main streets in our town. There I had a favorite seat on the curbstone in front of Mr. Hicks' grocery store where I watched the marvels of the day go by. There were still a few horses used for work in those days and they fascinated me. One day I watched the milkman stop his wagon at a watering trough across from Mr. Hicks' grocery in front of the shoe factory. This public facility, even then a relic of past days, was one of three left in the town. A second one was on the main public square where it served the downtown horse traffic in earlier times. The third trough, now empty, was in the middle of the square on Market Street and in times, not so long before my time, satisfied the thirst of the farmers' horses when they brought their produce to market.

The milkman was patient, and after wiping sweat from his own forehead with a big red bandanna handkerchief, moved to his horse's head and waited until his animal satisfied his thirst. And then, with the same bandanna, whisked the flies away from his horse's watering eyes. I was fascinated by this animal and every time I heard the milkman and his horse plodding down the street, I ran to my curbstone and admired this wonderful creature that God put on this earth.

I paid a penalty for my runaway excursions and finally, much to my young embarrassment, mother tied me to the porch railing with a clothesline rope. My days of free wandering were over.

Another time a circus came to our town. Bill posters did their job well, and gaudy, bright colored posters were pasted on every empty building and all of the available fences. Best I can recall, it was the Sells-Floto Circus. The circus posters advertised a grand street parade, and when the big day did arrive, the streets were full of curious and excited bystanders waiting for the parade to begin.

It was a hot day in August 1929, when the circus finally arrived. This time Father and Mother tended me in front of Mr. Hicks' grocery as the circus paraded by my special place.

As we watched down the street for the parade to start, we saw the first of the procession come into view. It was a fancy four wheeled buggy, painted snow white and trimmed in gold. It was pulled by two richly colored sorrel horses, their flaxen manes and tails glistening like gold in the sunlight. The rig was driven by an impressive looking man dressed in the exact livery of a fancy coachman. He wore a bright red coat with shiny brass buttons, a tall black stovepipe hat, white britches and tall black riding boots. To add to his elegance, he had a mustache, the ends waxed to fine points that were turned up in a fancy curl. Obviously he was a man of importance in the circus, maybe even the owner! Riding in the buggy with him were two beautiful young circus ladies dressed in gorgeous spangled dresses. Their long curls of hair were the same color as the horse's manes and tails, and they waved to the crowd as they passed along the way. This first display amazed the public. Could all of the circus be this grand?

Following the leading buggy, great parade wagons pulled by Percheron horses, their gray coats dappled with darker spots, creaked along the street. The proud drivers expertly handled their teams as clowns followed and brought laughs with their painted faces. Uniformed musicians riding high on top of the richly carved and gilded band wagon filled the air with brassy marching tunes. Next came elephants shuffling along the hot brick pavement. They and fancy high stepping riding horses stirred up the street dust. These animals captivated all, young and old alike. And then the very last wagon came into view belching steam from its pipes and filling the air with the loud boisterous music of the calliope. As the calliope signaled the end of the parade, the street watchers fell in behind it and, like rats following the piper, followed the parade to the circus lot. The tented circus was in its heyday—a great part of Americana. A young person like me couldn't help but be absolutely fascinated by it all, especially the horses!

§   §   §

In the late twenties my home town, like the rest of America, was in the grip of a great depression. World War I hadn't been over very long, and the scars were still there but gradually fading away. The Depression was like an epidemic and the entire nation suffered. The stock market collapsed and most citizens were financially in a bad way. It caused nearly everyone discomfort and most had to change their lifestyles. Our President, Herbert Hoover, a brilliant man, took the brunt of the blame. By the late twenties and early thirties many bread winners were out of work or took drastic cuts in pay just to salvage their jobs. Soup lines for the temporarily indigent were common; some sold apples or pencils on the street corners just for enough money for food. Prostitution flourished; the oldest profession in the world was a quick way for many girls to make money. Prohibition kept the country dry but moonshining and the speakeasies flourished. Kids my age were growing up in a new kind of society.

As I sat on my curbstone in front of Mr. Hicks' grocery store, on rare occasions the sound of an airplane flying over our town would catch my attention. Most everybody was curious about these machines, and after one flew over, it became the main topic of conversation. "Lucky Lindy" Lindbergh just a short time before flew his airplane, *The Spirit Of Saint Louis*, across the Atlantic Ocean to France. This new American hero whetted the American people's interest in this great invention. I am sure I heard people saying, "Yep, the flying machine is the transportation of the future." But in my young mind the airplane would never replace the horse.

§   §   §

Nineteen thirty three was an election year and the voters, tired of hard times, elected a new president, Franklin D. Roosevelt. He inherited Hoover's Depression, and in his weekly broadcast radio talks called "Fireside Chats," he promised prosperity and economic recovery. He began by creating the Works Progress Administration, the Public Works Administration and the

Civilian Conservation Corps. These quickly became known as the WPA, the PWA and the CCC, everyday terms in those times. They employed thousands of workers and slowly things looked better. But in spite of these hard times, America was progressing. Most people by this time had a radio and a telephone in their homes. But to a kid like me, six years old, who cared? I wanted a pony or a horse, but when I begged for one, my father had a stock answer, "We can't afford it." And then he generally added, "Where would we keep a pony?"

With the improving times most people eventually got an automobile. The old stables and elegant carriage houses were now called "garages" and instead of housing the once proud equine, the automobile—a cold piece of metal—sat in its stead. My father was a civil engineer and through the Great Depression worked for the WPA. As times improved he and Mother built a house at the edge of town. I grew up in that house and by this time I could see that we had a place for a pony. But once again , according to Father and what with a new baby brother, " . . . we couldn't afford it."

The horse topic eventually faded away and after a while we got a cocker spaniel. One day he got a runny nose and then his eyes matted shut with yellow pus infection. We took him to Dr. Karr, the veterinarian in our town. He examined the dog and told us he had distemper. He also told us it was a deadly disease in young dogs and he doubted if the dog would recover. We took our dog home and faithfully gave him the medicine the veterinarian had prescribed. For a while it looked like my spaniel would survive. Then one day he had a fit. His teeth chattered and copious amounts of frothy saliva poured from his mouth. His head was drawn back and he collapsed. It was a frightening experience and Mother was afraid the dog was mad. But Dr. Karr assured her he was not mad, though he continued to be doubtful about our dog's recovery. Even though he seemed better, he continued to have more and more frequent seizures. Each consecutive one was longer and more violent. Karr said there was nothing more he could do and mercifully euthanized my pet. Once again I saw the sadness of a sick, helpless animal and death. My mother cried and tried to comfort me. I was crying too.

Some months later an itinerant photographer knocked on our front door and asked my mother if she would like to have her children's picture taken on his pony. I looked out the door and sure enough standing at the street curbing was an absolutely gorgeous spotted pony. It was resplendent with a fancy bridle and a small western saddle. Mother thought this would get my mind off the death of my dog. It did just that but reignited the flame for getting my own honest-to-goodness pony. As I sat on that pony for my portrait, I was a king, a knight and a cowboy all at the same time! It had been worth waiting all of this time just for this one moment — or at least I thought it was.

§ § §

The seeds had been planted. In time they would mature, leading me to a career in veterinary medicine.

THE FORTIES

THE THIRTIES STRUGGLED TO AN END. THE ECONOMIC DEPRESSION THAT gripped our country was over. The destruction and devastation of the great flood of '37 that swept the Ohio River Valley, and my home town, had been cleaned up. Both left very bad memories. Franklin Roosevelt, now in his second term as President, guided our nation to a better economy. The new decade, eventually called "The Roaring Forties," was ready to begin. It would prove to be a powerful time that affected most Americans' lives, mine included.

§ § §

Four periods marked my life during those years: growing up, World War II, living through lean days in college and establishing my new family. But first I must finish telling about my growing up because it sets the stage for the molding of my life.

I grew up and went to grammar school just three blocks down the hill from our house. I wasn't very fond of school but attended and did as well as any boy who had his mind on other things. I really preferred listening to the popular radio shows such as Jack Armstrong, The All American Boy or Little Orphan Annie. Annie had a shaggy dog named Sandy whose reply to every statement was, "Arf." One of my favorite shows was an early country music show hosted by Mr. Bradley Kincaid. He was a good singer and his theme song, "In The Hills Of Old Kentucky," was a catchy tune. I just imagined him strumming his guitar and looking longingly into the hills of that fabled land.

Kentucky was a mysterious place to most youngsters. Many tales about the early pioneers, Simon Kenton and Daniel Boone, were told and retold. My town was situated at the mouth of the Scioto River where it empties into the mighty Ohio. This is the very place that most of the Indian fighting and early settler's adventures took place. Every morning after mother started me toward school, I would walk down the hill humming Kincaid's theme song and at the same time look straight ahead and see those tall, steep, wooded hills just across the Ohio River. In my mind they were waiting to be re-explored.

I eventually made it to high school, never giving up my request for a horse or a pony. Finally Father consented and we did get a horse, a pretty sorrel mare. Her owner, a local horse trader, loaned her to us for the winter, saving money by not having to feed her. After all those years of pleading, I finally had a horse. We built a stable behind the automobile garage and now I was truly a knight—without armor! In the spring that horse went back to its rightful owner. Soon after that, Father purchased a horse for Mother and a nice big pony for me. We only had room for one in our stable so Mother's new horse was stabled at the Selby horse barn about a mile from our house. He also bought a smaller older pony for my little brother, and managed to find a corner in the garage for this one. We were now, as the saying goes, "horse poor," and with a horse and two ponies, we became better acquainted with Dr. Karr, the veterinarian.

In the summers I worked for my father on one of the surveying crews he employed, but every evening, and other times I didn't work, I spent my time with my animals. I gave little thought to the future. I was satisfied with what I had.

Four years of high school passed quickly. The Forties had arrived! We growing-up young men dated the girls, learned to smoke cigarettes and taste beer and whiskey. These, good or bad, were the trends of the times for our generation. To our parents' dismay, we swam in the dirty Ohio River. We took our square ended, flat-bottom, wooden johnboats to the middle of the river and rode the huge waves created by the churning paddle wheels that moved the steamboats up and down the Ohio. Still, the clouds of war were forming, and we all watched as Hitler overran and conquered the small European countries. Many said we were fortunate to be a neutral country and stay out of the fighting, but it was inevitable that sooner or later we too would go to war.

One day in my last year of high school, Father came to me and asked me what I intended to do after graduation. Without a bit of hesitation I said, "Dad, I am going to be a veterinarian just like Dr. Karr."

You would have thought the world was coming to an end as he exploded with, "Who in the hell ever heard of a horse doctor making a living?"

"But that's what I really want to do." Without another word, he turned and walked back to the house, muttering some things I did not hear. That evening at the supper table he brought up the subject again and suggested I should go to an engineering school and follow in his footsteps.

"Son, beyond a shadow of doubt we are going to be involved in this war and if you go to engineering college, you will probably get a deferment and not have go." The discussion was ended. Mother looked at me with sympathy, I looked toward the stable and my horse.

I finally reconciled myself that maybe engineering was the path to follow, but my heart was certainly not in it. As I have told others since then, "Father committed me but I did not like it."

Fall came and, armed with a slide rule and other school supplies, I was put on a train and shipped to Virginia Polytechnic Institute to become an engineer. I tried to like it but each day got worse. It was a military school. That part I liked, but the calculus, chemistry and mathematics dropped me in my tracks. I simply had no desire to survey land and build roads and bridges.

On off days and after my classes and military duties were over, to forget the rigors of the day, I would go to the college farm and watch the cows and horses grazing in the pastures. One day, leaning across the fence watching a cow lick her new calf, I heard an airplane and recalled the days when I was small and people talked about Lucky Lindy Lindbergh. They said he was as, ". . . free as a bird in the sky." I wanted to be free too.

§   §   §

In December 1941, the Japanese attacked Pearl Harbor. We were finally at war. I was eighteen years old now and considered myself capable of making up my own mind as to my future. My decision was made. I walked out of VPI, hitch-hiked to Roanoke and enlisted in the Army Air Corps Aviation

Cadet Program. In a short time I was called to active duty. Finally I was out of that school and, best of all, out of engineering.

The military service was certainly a different experience for every American boy and girl that served the U.S. during those times. At the beginning all of us were just young, green kids. We went through all kinds of hell in the training camps. We mixed with all kinds of good and bad people of all colors. The training system homogenized these differences and before long we all worked as one for a common cause. The rigors of training were hard, but most made it and did their jobs with pride .

My choice was aviation and what a joy it was to be part of those that did just that—fly! I matriculated through the Texas flying schools and learned my job well, graduating as a second lieutenant and proudly wearing the silver wings of an army pilot. My desire was to become a bomber pilot. I had my heart set on flying a B-17 or a B-24—both new, big and awesome flying machines.

But the quota for bomber pilots at that time was full, and since most decisions were made by the military for you, I learned to fly C-47 cargo airplanes. They were nicknamed "biscuit bombers" and were not nearly as glamorous as the big four engine jobs that were dropping real bombs on the enemy. These cargo aircraft were often jokingly refered to as music boxes—someone said when you opened the door and learned to fly them, they all played *The Song Of India!*

In short order, sure enough as the song implied, I was sent to India to haul supplies to the fighting men in the jungles of Burma and the mountains of China. Under these trying circumstances, it didn't take long for those green kids of a few previous months to become men. Besides air-dropping supplies, we sometimes landed our airplanes in muddy, tiny airstrips hacked out of the jungle by those waiting for our goods.

The war progressed. China needed American goods to survive, so we were ordered to fly our cargos from India across the Himalaya Mountains to China. The air route became known as "The Hump" and was notorious for its unkindness to airmen and their airplanes. The weather was absolutely horrible all of the time. During the monsoons it rained incessantly. Thunderstorms and the weather were one of our enemies—the other, the Japanese Air Force. Both downed and killed many of my friends and fellow pilots.

On December 14,1944, I was flying a drop mission to the troops fighting on the Burma-China border. The Japs were watching and we were attacked by Japanese fighter airplanes. Of the six C-47s involved, three escaped, but not undamaged. I managed to get away from the fighters and landed at an airfield north of the drop target. My frantic radio calls were acknowledged, and when I landed there was a crowd of anxious airmen, a fire truck and an ambulance, anticipating a catastrophe. At the edge of the airfield was a group of soldiers leading a pack train of mules! This was a unit of the veterinary corps, and when the adrenalin of my misfortune returned to a proper level, I had the chance to talk to one of those veterinarians. I told him about my determination to pursue his profession. He laughed and said, "Hurry up and then you can lead this damned mule." He and his unit, satisfied my crew and I were OK and at a word from one of the other officers, left with their long-eared charges, walking down the road toward the fighting.

I was fascinated by the animal population. The tea plantation we lived on was hacked from the jungle, and the area teemed with wildlife. Monkeys filled the trees; birds of all colors, particularly parrots, were everywhere; and tigers, elephants, leopards and jackals roamed through the area of our tea plantation homes. The natives worked the rice fields with water buffalo and the thin, humped back Brahma sacred cows wandered aimlessly through the streets and along the roads. When I lived in Sylhet, our first airstrip home, there was a colony of monkeys that lived in the tree that supported my house, a bamboo basha. On days when I wasn't flying, I sat for hours watching the monkeys watch me!

Somehow, with the blessing of God, good training and military discipline, and a lot of good luck, I did my tour and was sent back to the U.S.A. and a new beginning.

§   §   §

Home from the war, I made my plans for the future. The first thing I did was to ask the girl I wrote the letters to from India, Mary Helen Feyler, to marry me. Her father, a dental surgeon and one time ranking dental officer in the United States Army, approved at once. Her mother was in tears and with the opinion that we just couldn't survive and go to school at the same time. My mother added her thoughts and agreed with Mrs. Feyler that it couldn't be done. Mary Helen's dad said, "Let 'em alone. They will be a success." We were married in December 1945.

The second thing I did was to apply to the Ohio State University for enrollment in their College of Veterinary Medicine. I started back to school that fall, studying the courses that would qualify me to go on to veterinary college if and when I would be accepted.

Mary Helen and I found a one-room apartment, the kind you share the bath with six male students and a kitchen that left a lot to be desired. We painted the walls, patched the leaky sink and got rid of the cockroaches that ruled the roost in the kitchen. I found a job for after school hours working for the state highway department. Mary Helen typed term papers for students, and with the meager income from these two jobs and a small pittance from the government, we began married life.

All was not bliss. No sooner had we done a major overhaul and debugging of our one-room palace, than we were evicted! The landlord said he could get more money by renting to single students! We moved, this time closer to the university. We fixed this apartment up too with paint and polish, repairs and decorating. It looked pretty good. Again we were evicted. Reason? The landlord decided she could rent our rooms to male students, crowd two or more together and make more money.

One of my classmates, Bill Bechdolt, bought a house ten blocks south of the university, and we agreed to rent the upstairs. Our rent payment made his house payment and we both had quarters for the rest of our time at Ohio State. We painted and decorated this place too, and all looked good until one day the stove collapsed and simultaneously the ice box bottom rotted out and fifty pounds of just-bought ice crashed to the floor! Both appliances managed to give up the ghost at the same time; this was a bad situation when you were living on nothing. Finally Mary Helen's father said he would buy us a stove, and we went to Lazarus in Columbus and bought a refrigerator "on time."

School days were fun but they were hard times. It took a while to learn how to study again and it took some doing to learn how to make ends meet financially. Recreation was what we made for ourselves. We fished on warm days in the Olentangy River. On the cold days we just stayed home. Our big splurge was a once-a-year affair to a stage show at a downtown theater. We saved every scrap of change in a coffee can for that day. In three years we attended *Harvey*, with Joe E. Brown, and Edward Grieg's *Song of Norway*, both wonderful shows.

Landlord Bill's dad was a boisterous barber. He and his wife came every weekend with groceries, a pork heart and a case of beer. Sometimes they brought shrimp. Donna, Mary Helen and Mrs. Bechdolt were the cooks. They pressure cooked the pork hearts with pickling spices and soaked the shrimp in vinegar. We stuffed ourselves with this food and washed it down with beer.

We studied hard, kept a horse skeleton under the bed and eventually got to be upper-classmen. We were learning. Bechdolt worked in Hans Mueller's grocery store for his groceries. In my time off from my job I painted the inside of Hans' store. I took those wages out in groceries too. One day Mr. Meuller asked me if I would paint his house. He told me where it was and I agreed after riding the streetcar north of the university a few miles and looking it over. This was a large, white, two-story frame house with dormers on four sides of a black peaked roof and a porch across the front of the house.

Hans bought the paint and I worked all summer long scraping paint and re-coating his wooden house. Toward the end of summer, I was proud of what I had done and was through all but the dormer above the porch roof in the front of the house. I was down to one day's work and climbed the ladder from the porch roof to the main roof. Carefully I painted the front and then, staying ahead of the sun so the glare from the fresh white paint didn't blind me, I moved to the side. That side painted, I crawled around and painted the back side. One more side and I was done. As I worked my way around to the final side, the paint bucket slipped on the roof and turned over, spreading glaring white paint on Mr. Mueller's midnight black roof! I grabbed all the rags I had, but the white paint just wouldn't come off. In a flash I had the answer. I climbed down the ladder to the porch roof, then down another to the ground and ran all the way to the corner to a hardware store and bought a can of the cheapest black paint I could get. Hurrying back I climbed to ladder to the top of the porch and carrying my can of black paint, went on up the other ladder to the dormer and the now black and white roof. I opened my can of black and painted over the white spilled paint. To this day Mueller has never known anything was wrong. He thanked me for my good work, we settled up what he owed me with groceries and as a bonus threw in a case of beer! That evening after he closed his store he came to our house and ate pork hearts and helped us finish the beer.

Days in the clinic were wonderful for those of us who aspired to be animal doctors. We quickly assimilated new ideas and learned how to handle our mistakes. One day Bechdolt and I were assigned to the horse and cattle ward. As I walked down the aisle toward my patient, I saw Bill trying to take a long-horned Hereford cow's temperature. Bill was on one side of the partition, reaching around toward the cow's rear end with a thermometer. Now right there I figured I knew how to take a cow's temperature and Bill sure wasn't doing it the way Dr. Karr in Portsmouth showed me. With prideful authority I walked up and said, "Bill, give me the thermometer and I will show you how you are supposed to do this."

He never hesitated, handed me the small glass rod and backed away waiting to see what was going to happen next. Well, it happened. Before I could even get close to the cow she kicked at me, and as I crowded closer to keep from being hurt, she tried her best to get me down and gore me with those long sharp horns. This animal was a crazy killer. Somehow I managed to reach up and pull myself up the wall, hand over hand, with the help of some chain linked fencing that separated the stalls. By now there were grooms, students and teaching doctors with ropes, clubs and pitchforks all there trying their best to get me away from that crazy cow. Bill Bechdolt just smiled because he knew all along just how mean that cow really was. "Are you all right?" he asked. I assured him that they only thing hurt was my ego. The case was never mentioned again.

The summer between our junior and senior years, Mary Helen and I went to my home town Portsmouth. Mary Helen was pregnant, the baby due in August. I went to work for Dr. Karr who had turned out to be my best friend and my biggest booster. I learned a lot from Karr, and one of the biggest lessons was how to get along with clients. He made arrangements with most of the farmers to let me do their work when his work load got heavy, assuring them if I got in any difficulty, I was to call him and he would be there as soon as he could. It worked very well, the farmers indulgently realizing what a help I was to Karr and what experience I was getting. There were many exciting times that summer. I learned that rabies was one of the biggest problems we had in our area, and probably saw more rabid animals that one summer than a veterinarian of today's culture will ever see in a lifetime. I learned how to practically handle hogs and the cow and horse cases that came up everyday. It was a wonderful internship that no money could ever buy. Karr and I divided our time at work. One day he would stay in the office and I would make the farm calls—all the time under his supervision. The next day we would switch. I stayed in the office with John, his excellent lay helper.

On August 15 I got a phone call from one of the dairies. They had a heifer in labor and could I, ". . . come right now?" Mary Helen was having some infrequent labor pains and I told my caller I would try to get there later in the morning. I took my wife to the hospital. Her labor pains were becoming more frequent: I was concerned of course about her but also about the farmer who was expecting me at any time. Mary Helen realized what was happening and told me to go take care of the cow, and I promised I would be right back. I drove to the farm, delivered the calf and then hurried back to the hospital and my laboring wife. While I had been attending my patient, Mary Helen's doctor was attending her and delivered for us a baby daughter. We named her Teresa Lynn.

We went back to school that fall and realized that we were about to fulfill my goal, a degree in veterinary medicine. We discussed where we would go to practice, considering several places including northern Indiana and at an opposite extreme, Rome, Georgia.

While I was working for Dr. Karr at the Scioto County Fair in Lucasville, I met a man from Ashland, Kentucky, who showed fancy Hereford cattle. His name was Henri Riekert. Mr. Riekert asked me where I was going after I got out of school and I told him we were undecided, mentioning Georgia and Indiana. He insisted we come to Ashland and visit him to talk about the possibilities of locating there. Later as time permitted we did go visit Henri and found that a committee had been formed to entice me to come to eastern Kentucky. They needed a veterinarian; the last of the two who had been there for years had recently died. I told him that we would make the final decision come the next spring before we graduated in June.

The decade was over. The forties were past history. It was time to look at the future. The seeds of the thirties had been planted and now, with graduation just six months away, they were about ready to germinate.

§ § §

A new decade began and on June 5, 1950, I became a college graduated Doctor of Veterinary Medicine. After much discussion and soul searching, Mary Helen and I decided we would settle in Ashland, Kentucky, where we were so much wanted. Mr. Riekert and his committee assured me they would back my venture with moral support and help me establish the practice. I also had family ties there that would help us get established and, as I jokingly remarked some time later, ". . . nobody knew anything bad about me!"

Three days after graduation, with a partially paid-for Plymouth automobile, three hundred dollars cash, a young wife and a new baby, we moved to Kentucky, Bradley Kincaid's theme song, "In the Hills Of Old Kentucky," resounding in the back of our minds.

NEW GROUND

COUNTRY FOLKS USE THE TERM "NEW GROUND" WHEN THEY START A GAR-
den or sow a crop on land that has never been cultivated before.
The land first has to be cleared of trees, brush and rocks and other obstacles,
then it has to be plowed and made ready to plant. There is a lot of hard work
fixing this new ground, but when the crops are harvested, it is worthwhile.
I like to think of our move to Kentucky as "fixin' new ground."

It didn't take long to get acquainted with our new home and our neighbors. Mary Steele and her husband, Harry, lived across the street and they
went out of their way to introduce us to people and show us around the area.
Later Harry confided that he and his wife had worried if, "those two kids
could make a living by doctoring animals."

In spite of the primitive beauty, honesty and character of the people
found in most of eastern Kentucky, the hill country did have some draw-
backs. We lived in an area stereotyped as Appalachia, or at least in the
foothills of it. Certainly we fit the picture. The region was cursed with the
lack of communication facilities, poor roads and inadequate educational
opportunities. It was over blessed with hill country politics.

Telephone service was scanty and there were just a few telephones out of
the city limits. The last phone was at the Kentucky State Police barracks,
on the main highway, south of town. The state police served me well. The
farmers would drive to their office and have the dispatcher relay their mes-
sages to me. The same was true in the surrounding towns. The client would
go to town, use a public phone and call the police office. The message was
always promptly passed on to me. Of course I cultivated the friendship of
these helpful law officers and even to this day, now almost fifty years later,
when someone inquires about a veterinarian, the answer is always the same:

"Call Doctor Martin." Two or three years went by with this primitive communications system but eventually rural phone lines served much of the area.

Electrical service was also near non-existent in the rural areas, and most farm folks lighted their homes and barns with kerosene lamps.

Our roads were primitive. What there were simply followed the old paths and cow trails, taking the path of least resistance over the hills and through the valleys. There were only two paved main roads, US 60 toward Lexington and US 23, wandering laboriously south into the real mountain counties. The county roads were graveled, when it was available, and any road off these could at times be impassable.

Local politics was good and bad. Professional politicians hung on to their jobs with the tenacity of a biting bull dog, making their own rules and in some cases lining their pockets far above their meager salaries. Those who didn't help themselves to the cash, wallowed in the small town puddles of authority, like hogs on a sunny day.

Education, or at least the formal kind, for the rural dwellers was just fair; the urban teaching just slightly better. All Kentucky schools were down on the list of educational rankings. The rural population had its paradoxes. Some in our county had a good education, even college degrees. These were mostly held by ladies who went to the mountain colleges and studied to be school teachers. Other women were content to follow in the family lifestyle and let happen what would! The scant education was part of Appalachia, and with this lack of formal teaching came hill folks' ways and superstitions. It's not my intent to ridicule these people or make issue of these things, but nevertheless they were there. Many of the old fashioned or even superstitious practices went a long way back and involved the care of animals. If we were going to "make a living," as Harry Steele said, we would have to introduce my future clients to modern veterinary medicine. I started my self-styled education program the very first day we moved to Kentucky. It was going to be hard work, even harder than "breakin' new ground!"

§ § §

Our original plans were to rent a house to live in and build a modern veterinary office. It didn't work that way. Houses to rent were out of our price range and those we could afford were not fit to live in! Mrs. Phillips, the widow of a veterinarian who died in 1948, solved our problem and offered to rent me her husband's office for twenty-five dollars a month. She also agreed to call all of her husband's old accounts and tell them we were here. It was scary to think of that much money going out each month just for rent, but we had no choice. We also managed to borrow enough from the bank to make a down payment on a new house. The payments on the house were forty-two dollars a month—we were indeed indebted even before we got the first client! It was certainly an incentive to work hard.

Those early days were eventually rewarding but often frustrating. On some days all I would get were phone calls wanting to know, "Doc, how much do you charge?" or , "Do you just doctor dogs and cats or are you a 'real vet' who looks at cows and hogs and horses too?" Patiently I tried to appease them all.

I had no more settled in and put up my 'shingle,' as the old saying goes, when a man came to my office and asked me to come to his place and look at his cow. Before he spoke, he looked down at the floor—in an almost embarrassed way, apparently trying to avoid looking me in the face, he said, "Doctor, my name is Walter Kuzee and I got me a problem. I need you bad, can you come hep me?"

"Yes sir," pleased at getting a client, "What's your trouble?" Looking up from the floor, he stammered and said, "My cow's dead and I think I need your hep." Before I could get directions to his place, he said, "Iffen you kin come right now, you can just foller me home."

I followed Mr. Kuzee's car out to the country and eventually turned off the paved road onto a narrow, rough gravel road. By the time we reached his farm, I was covered with dust and roasting hot from the June sun. We drove into the barnyard. As he got out of his car, he turned to me and said, "I'll be right back, gotta tell the missus we're here."

The cow was sure enough dead, lying on her back and bloated like a big blimp. Her legs were pointed straight up from her puffed-up body and she looked like she would explode any minute! Green flies swarmed all over her.

In one corner of the barnyard, tucked under the shade of an old oak tree, was a shed, the cow's protection from the weather. Along one side of this building, under the speading branches of the tree, was a large log. I walked over and sat down on the log, appreciating the cooling shade, and waited for my client to come back. In just a minute or two he was back and when I looked up from my shady seat, I asked him to tell me about the cow. I moved over and he sat down on the log beside me.

I asked some questions about the cow's illness and what symptoms he saw before the cow died. Kuzee stood up and began telling me what he saw. "Mr. Doctor," he said, "she stood humped up in her back." He went through the motions of humping his back, and then he added, "That old cow walked real stiff-like, and grunted every step she took." Still humped up in his back like he said his cow was, now he shuffled off in a stiff legged gait, uttering a grunt with every step he took. Appearantly waiting for me to get the clear picture, he put his hands up to his throat as he continued, "A few days after I noticed her ailin', she got swolled under her neck." This man certainly did know how to describe dramatically what he saw. Needless to say, I was really being entertained as well as being informed!

He sat back down on the log with me and, still avoiding looking me straight in the eye, he finally said, as if almost daring to ask the question, "Doctor, do you believe in witches?"

I almost fell off of the log in disbelief at this statement. Now this man really had my attention! Gathering all of the tact I could muster on such a short notice at such a question, I hesitated for a second or two and replied, "Well," I paused again trying to come up with a suitable answer, "I don't really think I do."

Kuzee was quick to come back with, "Well, Doc," not being nearly so formal with my title and appearing to be greatly relieved, "I reckon I don't either." This time he looked me straight in the eye! I'm not sure I believed him.

After giving me the history, he looked up and pointed to a house about a half mile away, up on the hillside. He asked me if I saw it. I told him I did.

"Doc, they's an old woman that lives there that folks don't know much about." Now I was at complete attention because I suspected the witch business was about to come up again. Walter continued, "Her and my neighbor down the road got into it 'cause he couldn't pay her some money he borrowed from her—told her she would have to wait 'cause he was laid off from the railroad shops." Walter went on to tell me that his neighbor had a hog die and he believed that the old lady had hexed his hog over the money debt!

Fascinated with this almost unbelievable story, I wondered what trouble Walter had with this woman. In the next breath he said, "She's on me too 'cause this old cow kept gettin' through the fence into her garden. I kept a-patchin' the fence, but the old bobwire is rotten." His colloquialisms rang out loud and clear!

By this time I had the case pretty well figured out and turning to Kuzee I said, "Let's examine the cow and if necessary, I'll do an autopsy and we'll find out what killed her." He agreed and we both got up from our shady seat and walked over to the dead cow.

I went through my examination, at the same time trying to keep the literally thousands of flies out of my face. I finished my initial investigation and went to the car for my post-mortem instruments. Coming back, I explained to Walter I thought the cow had swallowed a piece of metal, possibly a piece of the rotted barbed wire from the lady's garden fence. I further explained that the "bobwire" had punched a hole through her stomach and then into her heart. I described how the heart and front of the stomach were close together, telling him this was a common condition.

"How come her to be so swolled under her neck iffen it were her heart that was ailin' her?"

"That's easy, when her heart went bad, the circulation went bad too. She had heart dropsy just like some people do." My answer seemed to satisfy him and he asked no more questions.

I made a big bold cut into the cow's greatly distended stomach, quickly trying to get out of the way to avoid being soaked with stomach contents and overcome by rank smelling stomach gasses as they exploded from the cut in the bloated carcass. I didn't quite make it and in an instant I was covered with green, foul smelling, sticky, partially digested, grass and cow feed! As the gas and the nasty green mess rushed out, the cow deflated like a punctured balloon. I manually unloaded a lot more stomach contents and shoved my arm as far as it would go up into the front part of the stomach and searched for the foreign body that I knew was there. While feeling for the wire, or whatever it was, the flies were swarming all over me and my smelly, dirty clothes. Looking up, I asked Walter to, "Go to the house and get some soap and water and a towel."

"Doc, the well pump is busted. You'll have to wash in the branch behind the barn." He added, "Would a clean feed sack be OK for a towel?" I grunted something affirmative and went on with my work. Sweat rolling off of me, stinking from the green juices of the cow's rumen and covered with flies, I finally found the trouble. As I suspected, a piece of barbed wire, about six inches long, had done its job punching through the stomach wall into the heart. With some difficulty I retrieved the foreign body and showed it to Kuzee. He seemed satisfied. I walked to the creek, or branch as Mr Kuzee called it, and washed myself, as best I could, in a water hole that was surrounded by cow droppings all swarming with hundreds of big green flies! The water felt good and as I dried my hands and face and arms on a feed sack, I wondered if I had convinced Walter it was the foreign body in his cow's heart and not the old lady's witchcraft that did his cow in.

I drove back to town and stopped by the house for a change of clothes and a quick shower to get rid of the dead cow odor. Briefly, I related the story to Mary Helen. She said in amazement, "You have to be kidding me!" I assured her I was not.

Kuzee wasn't alone when it came to witchcraft or superstitions, or more properly termed, hill country beliefs. It was the usual, rather than the unusual, to be called to look at a sick cow and find her tail bandaged with a rag. First thing most farmers did when a cow got sick was to feel for a soft spot close to the end of her tail. They called this ailment, "wolf-in-the-tail." If it was there, the farmer took his pocket knife and split the skin on top of the tail. Then he poured salt into the wound and wrapped it with the rag! Of course this hurt and the poor cow, stimulated by the pain, appeared more alert and did indeed move around better. I always thought the cows were trying to walk away from the pain.

"Holler horn." This was another ailment diagnosed by the farmer. What the symptoms were I didn't know, but it didn't take long for me to cease to be amazed when one day a cow owner told me he cured "his cow brute" when he held a spoon full of turpentine up to the cow's navel! Proudly he said,"Doc, she sucked it right up."

Cows also "lost their cuds." Not really—but most hill farmers thought they did. Most any systemic disturbance, particularly those involving the digestive tract, would cause the animal to stop the digestion process we called rumination. When the cow did not ruminate, she didn't regurgitate her partially digested food and she stopped chewing her cud. The cud normally was this regurgitated material that was rechewed and swallowed before digestion was completed. There were two homemade remedies for this. The treatment of choice was to catch a toad and force it down the animal's throat. If you couldn't find a toad, a greasy dish rag supposedly worked just as well!

Horse and mule practice had some hill country remedies too. The first time I was called to treat a case of "lampers," the farmer asked me to be sure and bring my hot iron. The malady was simply a swollen upper palate in a young horses's mouth when the colt cut its new teeth. It was not a disease, but a natural condition. The old-timers heated an iron rod, got it red-hot and seared the roof of the colt's mouth! I was shocked when I saw the first colt slobbering and suffering from this brutal treatment. The less harsh treatment was to rub the colt's mouth raw with a corn cob; harsh, but not quite as brutal! Over the years I solved this mayhem when I let it be known to the horse people, "Doc Martin had a new medicine for the lampers—give 3 tablespoonsful 3 times a day for 2 weeks." My colored water, laced with molasses, worked; tincture of time healed the swollen palates.

I soon realized educating my new Kentucky friends to accept modern day veterinary medicine would be a tremendous undertaking. And, like the farmer breaking new ground, my job would be time consuming and require a lot of hard work. I hoped it would eventually get results.

The Critter That Started It All

About two months after I opened my office, a man came to me and told me his name was Pidge Mohr. Mohr was a medium-sized, round-faced, pudgy fellow with a slightly receding hair line and pouty lips. His face looked like it hadn't seen a razor for at least two days. This man was wearing riding jodhpurs and smoking a cigarette that had burned down to where it almost burned his lips. Never removing the stub of the cigarette from his mouth he said, "I have a horse barn out at the edge of town where I board and train saddle horses." He coughed from the smoke and then went on to say, "I've got a horse that needs some dental work. When can you come look at him?"

"I'm about finished, how about in thirty minutes?" I tried to act that it was coincidence I was done with my work, but actually I didn't have anything else to do. "Tell me how to get to your barn."

"If you are coming that soon how about me waiting and, if you don't mind, we will go out there together." He lit another cigarette from the almost burned-out stub, and after I pointed to an ashtray, he stubbed out what was left of the first one and started puffing on the new one.

I agreed to going with him, and after I finished adjusting a splint on a dog with a broken leg, Mohr asked me about my background. He said he heard I liked horses and owned some at one time. I told him about my pony and the horses we had before the war. I also told him if I ever made any money I would like to have another horse. He jumped on that remark and said, "When you're ready for 'em, Doc, just let me know—I'll sell 'em to you."

I followed his car through a nice residential section of town and ended up at his place of business just at the city limits on a graveled road. Pidge's barn had fourteen box stalls—a horse in every one—a tack room and a

27

combination office and loafing room. Overhead was a big hay loft.

We walked down the aisle of the barn and Mohr told me about every animal and who owned it. I was impressed and hoped this visit would lead to a lot more business and a chance to be around horses again.

Stopping in front of one of the stalls, he pointed to the horse and said, "This is the horse I think has the bad teeth. When he eats he holds his head to one side and some of his food falls out of his mouth."

After snapping a lead shank to the ring in the halter, he led the horse out of the stall and fastened him in the cross ties in the aisle of the barn. I reached into the horses mouth, carefully grabbed his tongue with one hand, so he couldn't bite me, and with my other hand examined his teeth. This horse, about seven years old, had needle-sharp edges and points on the outside edges of his upper teeth that were cutting the inside of his cheeks when he ate. The lower arcade of teeth were worn to sharp points on the tongue side and these cut his tongue as he chewed his grain. I explained this to Pidge and he promptly told me, "Doc, I knew that before you looked in his mouth. You just fix 'em."

I got my newly chromed dental tools out of my car, asked for a bucket of water and rolled up my sleeves. I was ready for work. The stable boy brought me the water and Pidge helped me adjust the mouth speculum; once it fit, I opened the horse's mouth and let the ratchets on the speculum hold the horse's mouth open. Inserting the long handled float, really a fine toothed rasp on a long handle, I gently filed the sharp edges away. I explained, as I was doing this, that some operators were over zealous and removed more of the tooth than was necessary. Finished, I closed the speculum and dropped it and the float into the water bucket and, in the same bucket, washed my hands.

"OK, Pidge, you can put him away." I continued talking to him as I walked to the next stall and looked at another horse. "How come you to call me for this job?"

"I talked to Tom Hodge yesterday. He said you really knew your stuff about horses so I figured I would find out for myself." With that remark he reached into his shirt pocket, pulled out a pack of Camel cigarettes and lit a new one from the one still dangling from the corner of his mouth. He spit the old burned down stub out on the floor and ground it into the dirt with his foot. "Gotta be careful with fire around a barn, you know." As almost an afterthought he said, "How much do I owe you?"

"Five dollars." He paid off and then wanted to know if I would do all of his work and bill each horse owner for the services. I agreed to that, and this was the beginning of a long friendship and started me on my way to a good horse practice.

Driving back to my office I laughed to myself about the Tom Hodge episode that Pidge mentioned.

Just two days before, a small, well-dressed man, maybe fifty or fifty-five years old, had come to the office. Without any change of emotion, or any indication of friendliness, he told me his name was Hodge. His complaint was he had a young Tennessee Walking Horse that was having trouble eating and was losing weight. His direct question to me was, "Do you know anything about a horse?" After I told him I did in fact know something about horses, he softened a little and asked me when I could come to his barn and look at his colt. I made the appointment and he, and another man that was with him, walked out of my waiting room, got into a shiny big black Cadillac and drove away. I was not sure I was going to like this man.

I finished another little job I was doing at the office and was all set to go on a house call to treat a sick cat when the phone rang. The voice on the other end said, "Doctah Martin, I'm Billy Caldwell. I train walkin' horses for Tom Hodge. We got a young colt out heah with a sore mouth." Billy Caldwell with a drawl thicker than a Georgia pecan-pie filling went on to say, "We had anoth'a vet out heah yestaday, but he didn't know nothin' about a horse. Matter of fact, I even suggested to him our colt might have some caps, but that doctah said he didn't know what caps were." I informed Mr. Caldwell his boss had already talked to me and I had an appointment to look at the horse at eleven o'clock.

As soon as I hung up the telephone, I took my large animal disease textbook down from the book shelf and looked up the discussion on dental caps. I had heard about this condition but my memory was vague. I knew I had the jump on Tom Hodge but I had to be sure of my facts. The textbook described dental caps as baby teeth that were still cemented to the surface of the growing permanent teeth. They usually came off as the colt chewed its food. If for any reason they did not come off by nature, a stiff probe could be used and the caps pried or knocked off.

The Hodge stable was in a residential section that was sprinkled with several small back yard horse establishments. The barn was in Hodge's back yard, with a training track in the lot next to the house.

All in all, it looked like a neat, clean operation. There were only four stalls in this barn, but they housed four beautiful, well-groomed Tennessee walkers. Tom, his trainer, Caldwell, and another man, also employed by Hodge, were waiting for me. I carried my satchel of instruments and a clean pair of white coveralls to the barn. I set the bag down, was formally introduced to the young horse trainer and then pulled on my coveralls. Out of one corner of my eye I could see Tom waiting on my next move. It was matter of who headed the pecking order—me, or somber-faced Hodge.

I asked Billy to get the colt and fasten him in the cross ties and at the same time I asked the other man to get me a bucket of water. The colt was a good one, obviously well bred and expensive. I was to find out shortly that he was the son of the current world champion Tennessee Walking Horse! I added a small amount of disinfectant to the water and made a point of letting Tom Hodge know how important sterilized instruments were.

The stage was set. I had my audience; hopefully I would be a good actor! My fancy whites and my shiny and now disinfected instruments ready, I examined the colt's mouth. Blessings upon me—as I ran my hand along the molar teeth I discovered two flat baby teeth adhered to the new ones just protruding below the gums. Muttering to myself, but loud enough for Tom to hear, I said, "Yes sir, this colt has some caps on his teeth." Certainly—of course this vet knew what dental caps were! I watched Tom's expression out of the corner of my eye and knew I said just what he wanted to hear. While I was quietly savoring my little victory, Tom moved over to a cabinet fastened to the wall, opened the door, moved some horse linament and other stable supplies, and took out a bottle of bourbon whiskey. Without another word, he took the bottle cap off and had himself a drink. His frozen face managed a slight smile of satisfaction but I wondered if the smile was for John Martin, or "John Barley Corn!" That was the first time, and maybe one of the few times, I ever saw Tom Hodge smile. I tapped each tooth with the end of my long handled rasp and knocked the baby teeth loose. I reached into the colt's mouth and retrieved them, sloshed them in the bucket of water and handed them to Tom. I had won this match for sure and at the same time created a good horse client. Tom and his wife, Helen, became long lasting friends. Friends or not though, I was always a little guarded when I was around Mr. Tom.

Across the street from Hodge's place was another private stable. It was owned by Deck Sheets, a local auto agency dealer, whom Tom Hodge had told that I was really knowledgeable about horses.

I was soon called out there to worm his horses. The Sheets' barn had six stalls and the usual feed room and tack room, and I found that the three horses in this stable were all American Saddle Horses, a breed different from the Tennessee Walking Horses at the Hodge stable. A young neighbor boy who was waiting to help me brought out the first horse. I passed the stomach tube through the horse's nose into its stomach and poured down the liquid medicine. The kid stood there amazed as he watched me pass the tube and asked me if I could wait until he went across the street and get his friend so he could watch us work. I told him to hurry assuming he would only be gone a minute or so. Fifteen minutes later there was still no helper and by this time I was absolutely frustrated with this delay. I went to the house and told Mrs. Sheets what had happened. She called the boy's mother and an embarrassed Mrs. Sheets hung up the telephone and told me the mother had sent her boy to the grocery—it would be a while before he would be back! "Mrs. Sheets, I can't do this work by myself and if you want me to finish the job, just call me when you get me some help." I left in disgust.

Not more than ten minutes after I got back to my office, the phone rang and Mr. Sheets apologized for the inconvenience and made arrangements for me to meet him at his barn in the morning. I was there at eight o'clock and this time my helper was Sheets himself, business suit and all! We did the work; he paid me for two barn visits and my other work and gave me a five dollar tip. I accepted his apologies and felt really prosperous because five dollar tips were not part of that day and time.

In the same neighborhood, about three blocks away, was Mansbach's horse barn and two blocks from there, toward the Pidge Mohr barn, was the Hillendale Stables, a public stable that could house over one hundred head of horses! Fruitful territory indeed for a horse doctor if he could "get in."

That's just what occurred. Tom Hodge, Deck Sheets and Pidge Mohr did their work well and spread the word what a good horse doctor "Doc Martin" was. One horse job led to another, and in a short time I was busy treating everybody's horses in the area.

One day while I was working at the Mohrland Stable, a man came to me and introduced himself. This man was maybe thirty years older than I, with a soft look in his eye. Right away, I liked him. He held out his hand for a shake and said, "Doctor Martin, my name is Reese Wells," and before I could say anything he continued, "I've got a good mare road horse. All of a sudden while I was jogging her in the cart this morning, she went dead lame. I think maybe she broke a bone in her foot." Mr. Wells was obviously upset, almost to the point of crying. "Please come over to the big barn and look at her." I told him I would be there as soon as I was finished with Pidge's horse. With a grateful smile he thanked me and left.

A careful examination of the mare's foot made me think this horse had a fractured sesamoid bone. The sesamoids are small bones just above the hoof and are subject to fracture under extreme stress. Wells was terribly upset and he told me rather than destroy his mare—he called her Scarlet O'Hara of Gone With The Wind fame—he would go to any expense and effort to save her life. I told him I would try. I could see this was not a matter of money— he really loved this horse.

Back at my office I had some plaster of paris splints; a phone call to Curtis, my office helper, soon had him on his way to Hillendale with the supplies. I carefully bandaged the leg and applied the cast. While I was work- ing on this pretty mare, a crowd soon gathered to watch and see if there were really miracles in this world. After all, it was common knowledge that you shot a horse with a broken leg.

But we were going to try another plan. My instructions were for absolute stall rest for several weeks. I made no promises as to the prognosis, but told Wells I thought I could at least save Scarlet's life. Reese Wells and I both worked hard on this case. I changed the cast as it became necessary and Wells gave his animal all of the supportive treatment, such as using linea- ments, leg massage and tender loving care, he could. After a while the swell- ing started to leave and some weeks later, the ankle looked almost normal. One day I suggested to Reese that he start her back in training and see if the leg would hold up. I cautioned him to take it easy—just a little at a time and for Heaven's sake, I said, "Don't get carried away with speed." He promised he would do exactly as I said.

Scarlet O'Hara of the Gone With The Wind Stables went through the winter in good shape and in early spring was back in a full training program.

She went on to be a champion road horse year after year and she and her compassionate owner made road horse history. I had a real friend in Reese Wells, and his family too, for that matter, and every time Scarlet O'Hara was called before the judges for her blue ribbon, I always felt just a little bit proud for my part in her career. Also, for the records, this was really the beginning of an era in equine orthopedics that saw horses' bones fixed rather than, "Shoot em', Doc, his leg is busted!"

§   §   §

Not every equine case involved fancy show horses or high-stepping riding horses. The Kentucky highland area is full of coal, and in those days a lot of the coal was dug from deep mines, some hardly tall enough for a man to stand up in. The miner struggled with pick and shovel, and ponies hauled the coal out of the dark pits. Mine ponies were tough, hard workers, but not every pony was suited for the work. Some were too fragile and just couldn't physically handle the work, while others were too big to work in the low-ceilinged mine shafts. One mine owner was my client and the first time I saw his ponies, I felt sorry for them. They all had the hair worn off of their rumps below their tails, a result of the harness britchen rubbing them as they were pushed by the heavy mine wagons when they went down the steep inclines in the shafts. Their knees were swollen and scarred where they sometimes stumbled, struggling to pull the heavy, overloaded carts back up the same steep grade. Some had scars on their heads from hitting the low roof supports in the tunnels. But in spite of their equine occupational hazards, these little animals fared well and were given the very best of care. They were, at the time and in this type of mine operation, the sole means of moving the coal. I heard it said by many miners, "A good mine pony was worth his weight in gold!"

Down in Greenup County, the county just west of my town, the King Powder Company had a plant that manufactured gunpowder and explosive materials. The plant was scattered over a large area for safety reasons, separating one manufacturing area from another in case of an explosion. A rail system with horse-drawn rail wagons connected the different work sites, as the product progressed from one manufacturing station to another. In time I was employed as the veterinarian who cared for the draft horses that were indeed treated like kings! The stables were spotless, the animals well groomed, and no expense was spared in their care.

When I was called to the King Powder Company to treat an ailing horse, I had to go first to the office, turn in my cigarette lighter, pocket knife and any other object that could possibly strike a spark! I was issued special shoes whose soles were sewn on rather than nailed to the uppers.

All of the tools used by the plant workers were bronze, again a precaution against sparks and a devastating explosion. The wagon wheels were bronze and even the shoes the horse wore were bronze. This was a fascinating place to work and I stayed employed there until the plant was eventually abandoned. The horses were farmed out as "retirees," never to work another day in their lives. They earned that retirement.

Now there were other equine critters employed for draft purposes besides horses and ponies. Mules abounded in the hill country. I love a mule— at least some of them. One day Claude Groves came by my office and asked me if I could come by his place and put a mule to sleep so he could, ". . . tack some shoes on the son-of-a-bitch." Claude operated a saw mill and used his mule to pull logs out of the woods.

This mule, as the old-timers would say, " was broke to death." He was the best worker you ever saw until you tried to pick up his feet. Once you reached down toward a hoof he went absolutely nuts—striking at you and trying to bite and kick at the same time! As long as you didn't touch his feet, he was as gentle as a springtime lamb. Claude lived about a mile, as the crow flies, from my office and I told him I would be there shortly and give his mule an injection of a tranquilizer.

"Will that put the son-of-a-bitch to sleep?"

"Nope, Mr. Groves, this is a new drug and to explain it so you understand, it's like the critter sees the Devil across the road but when he's full of this medicine he doesn't pay any attention to him."

"To Hell with the Devil, I just want shoes on that damned mule. I'll be waitin' for you. Matter of fact, I'll have him tied to the electric pole down by the road."

At the appointed time, I drove out to Claude's saw mill and, sure enough, he had the mule tethered to the electric pole. I got the medical bag out of my car and filled a syringe with the tranquilizer. Claude held the mule's bridle with one hand and with his other grabbed and twisted the mule's ear to hold him still while I disinfected a spot over the animal's jugular vein and slowly injected the medicine. "It will take a few minutes for the medicine to work but you won't have any trouble now. These new miracle drugs work wonders." Claude paid me, I got back in my car and drove back to my office.

When I got back Curtis was standing in the doorway, telephone in hand, waiting for me. It was Claude on the line. I could hear him shout before I ever put the phone to my ear, "Doc, the damned mule went plumb crazy after you give him that shot—he even tried to climb the electric pole!"

I tried to calm Claude down and finally, when it was my turn to talk, I figured out the medicine had a reverse effect on this animal and instead of calming him down, it acted like a strong stimulant. I told him I would be right there.

We finally got a rope around the mule's neck and with effort got my twitch—a maddox handle with a small chain looped through the end of it, twisted around his nose to calm him down. Then I managed to get a needle into his jugular vein and started a bottle of chloral hydrate, a strong sedative, on its way. It didn't take long and Claude's pride and joy was sound asleep on the ground. Claude stood there and stared at the mule and I heard him one more time say, "You son-of-a-bitch." I wasn't sure if he was addressing me or his mule but since we are still good friends, I am sure he meant his log-puller. Later on Claude told me it took the mule about three hours to wake up, and he did indeed get the shoes tacked on him.

Horse traders, and Heaven knows Kentucky is full of them, helped me start my practice too. Late one warm summer evening Pidge Mohr and I were out in front of his barn admiring his new sign that expounded on the offerings of the Mohrland Stable. It was a good sign, and Pidge was very proud of it. As we stood back and looked at this art work, he said, "Doc, now I am really in business!" I appreciated how he felt because it was just a few months earlier when I hung out my shingle.

As we stood there and stared at the sign painter's work, a car pulled into the barn lot and a well-dressed—suit-and-necktie, just-proper-middle-aged-man got out and walked over to where we were standing. He never said a word until he had walked all around the sign and finally addressing Pidge he said, "Bless you, my boy, it looks like you spent your money wisely." Then he turned to me, held out his hand and added, "I am Reverend Fugate, you must be the new veterinarian the people at Hillendale are talking about." I shook his hand and told him I guessed I was.

Pidge stood there and laughed. "Doc, don't let the preacher," he used the term in a complimentary way, "fool you. He's as slick a horse trader as there is anywhere here in the hills!" Reverend Fugate smiled, turned to me and jokingly told me some people had little or no manners. At first I thought this man of the cloth might be out of his element, but when I learned he was a devoted clergyman as well as a lover of horses, I cast aside my doubts and smiled at my new acquaintance. Pidge spoke up and said, "We call this guy 'the Preacher' but he really is a pretty good guy." I am sure that the Reverend Fugate appreciated these kind words.

Fugate was an evangelist of some repute and was known all over the country for his ability to successfully conduct large tent revivals. Everybody liked him and his permanent smile and nearly everyone respected him. Once in a conversation he told me he served the Lord seven days and seven nights a week. He added, "Doctor, in my spare time I trade a horse or two."

Over a period of time we spent many hours talking about his religion and his church. He told me, after we really became friends, how he conducted his big tent meetings and raised large amounts of money for his church; he was a obviously a devoted man—truly a servant of the Lord.

And then of course the conversation got back to the horse business, particularly about his horse trading. He looked at me with that permanent fixed smile and with a slight twinkle in his eye he said, "Doctor Martin, tradin' for a horse is just like the church business. First, you show 'em the product. Then you haggle a while for the money."

"And finally," with an even bigger smile he said, "you deliver the goods." That remark gave me food for thought.

§   §   §

Several months went by, fall prettied up the woods and then winter hit us hard. We had lots of snow and most hill folks just sat around the fire and waited for the spring thaw. Considering the bad weather, business wasn't too bad. Cows and horses got sick and I stayed fairly busy. After the winter snows finally melted and the weather warmed up, the preacher called me one morning and said he wanted me to come to the Hillendale barn and look at a young horse. He said no more. I met him and as we walked down the aisle of the big barn he told me about a registered saddle horse gelding he thought would interest me. Up till now I hadn't really thought about buying a horse. Money was still pretty short and my big house and office payments made spare change hard to come by. But, the preacher had a captive audience—to make this story short—I gave him seventy-five dollars, he gave me the registration papers, and I owned a pretty three-year-old sorrel gelding that was just barely broke to ride. I was back in the horse business.

FOR BETTER OR WORSE

THE HOT DAYS OF OUR FIRST SUMMER IN KENTUCKY WERE COMING TO AN end and as fall approached, the nights began to cool down and the hills started changing color. When we got the chance, Mary Helen, baby Terri and I traveled every road in the county trying to get the lay of the land and enjoy our beautiful, newly adopted countryside. We didn't drive too fast and every time I saw a farmer we both waved at him out of the car window like he was a long lost friend! Something worked and one day one of my new dairy clients made the remark, "Doc, the first time I ever seed you, you and your missus retched out and woved at me from your car." It was good, being friendly, and apparently good business too!

These first months were rewarding. We made many friends and soon began to fit into the community. We were more than pleased with our decision to move to Kentucky. My horse practice was growing and the farm work, thanks to Henri Riekert and his committee, and my own hard work and good results, picked up momentum. By early autumn I was a regular working visitor to Cedar Knoll Farm, Henri Riekert's place, John Evan's Hickory Hill Dairy and bus line owner C.E. Fannin's cattle farm. Paul Pollitt, a realtor, was developing some real estate that formerly belonged to the Means-Russell Iron Works, just west of our town in the next county. He grazed his cattle on the empty land, soon to become an area of our community known as Bellefonte—named after an early iron furnace of bygone days. His cattle received my attention too. Henry Pope was the county extension agent and true to his word, "I'll sing your praises loud and clear if you come to our county," contacted all seventy-three of the dairy farms in the county and told them I was here. For a freshly capped veterinarian, this whole situation was beyond belief. I was ecstatic, and never gave any thought there were downsides to everything good. Then, quicker that a mule could kick you, some of the inconveniences of a veterinary practice began happening.

§　　　　　§　　　　　§

One morning about eleven o'clock, a young man and his woman came to the office and handed me a box of dead baby chickens! The man needed a shave and his shirt looked like it hadn't been washed for several wearings. His blue jean trousers were worn thin and the knees were dulled with dirt. One of his hip pockets bulged with a huge pouch of chewing tobacco. The other was filled with a heavy wallet fastened to his belt with a short chain. This seemed to be some sort of a badge of authority among a certain social class in this area. His woman presented a no better look, with her stringy, unwashed hair. It was obvious these people were not high on the social pecking system! The man spoke and, giving me a direct order, said, "Tell me what's killed them chicks." Our conversation was meager. The woman never said a word but kept a steady gaze at me while I conducted my autopsy. The man then said, "These are valuable chicks, I sure hope to hell you know something about fightin' chickens." Eastern Kentucky was a haven for chicken fighting and now, fifty years later, there are still a lot of roosters, "on the walk," as the chicken fighters say.

In spite of today's laws, I am sure the fights still go on. I autopsied the dead birds and gave my opinion. The man looked up at me, turned around to his woman and they walked out of my door without as much as a thank you. I followed them and told the man he owed me two dollars for my services. He never uttered a word and they got in their old pickup truck and drove away. I just couldn't believe what had happened. Here we thought the hill-folks were all great people but we found one of the bad apples in the barrel, and I was out the two dollar fee after having performed my services.

§　　　　　§　　　　　§

Just before noon on a hot September day, a big Cadillac stopped in front of the office. It was long, black as coal and shiny, revealing either its owners wealth or inflated ego. A well dressed lady almost running as she came up the driveway was carrying a very sick little dog. I held the door open for her and directed her toward the examination table in the next room. Once the small female poodle was on my examination table, I tried to get some health history about her dog. I continued talking to her while I was examining her pet. She mentioned her husband, who I assumed was the man waiting in the car, was with a large insurance company in our town, and that he held an executive position and was a very busy man. Then as an afterthought, glancing out toward the car, she added, "He is quite impatient too." This lady was gentle and caring, almost in tears over her little poodle's illness. I tried to present my best "bedside manners" and proceeded with my examination.

I listened to the dog's lungs and heart with my stethoscope, in an attempt to hear the audible vital signs of my patient. As I was going through my procedure, this nice lady looked at me and with a sad smile said, "Doctor, please save my dog. My friends tell me you're very good and are the most compassionate animal doctor they ever knew." Hearing these nice words from this distraught lady immediately boosted my ego.

I listened to my patient's lungs, and then, as I was just ready to take her dog's temperature, her husband charged into my office and never bothering to look at me, took his wife by her arm and in a sarcastic, demanding tone of voice said to her, "Bring your dog, we'll take her to Huntington to the vet up there. He knows a lot more than this one does!" The lady looked at me almost in as much disbelief as I was at her husband's remarks. Without a word, but with a look of sincere apology, she picked up her dog and followed her husband out to their car.

I have often wondered what goes on with people who are absolutely rude and have no respect for others. After this episode was over, I wondered to myself if he was more pleasant when he was trying to sell insurance. Thankfully, I never experienced a situation just like this again in all of the years I served my community.

As a final note to this story, the lady called later that same afternoon and apologized for her husband's actions. She told me to send her a bill for my office call. She also told me that her little poodle died before they ever got her to the other doctor. Maybe I wasn't the loser after all!

§　　　　　§　　　　　§

The days got shorter and the trees started shedding their leaves. The late fall and early winter cold rains made farm work uncomfortable. But I was happy, the practice was doing well and I took the weather and unpleasant things in stride.

Minx Salyers was one of my new clients. He lived about eight miles south of town. Minx was his real name and somehow, it fit him to a "T." He was a tall, thin, hollow-cheeked man. Under his eyes were heavy bags of dark skin that gave his eyes a permanent sag as if his cheeks were too heavy! I hardly ever saw him smile but when he did, you had to look hard to see a facial change. Minx was really not too old, but the strain of hard, lean years as a hill country farmer aged him in looks. He didn't have the greatest personality in the world and, at times, seemed a little belligerent, always on guard about something. Finally, like a mink animal, Mr. Salyers never missed anything. He was aware of the world around him and cautious about what he did, planning each move with some direction. He was typical of the Kentuckians of my area.

His standard attire, like most of the hill country farmers, consisted of blue bibbed overalls worn over an old army kakhi or a faded denim shirt usually bleached and frayed from frequent scrubbing. His pants legs were always tucked into the tops of knee-high black rubber boots. His uncut, thinning hair was usually covered by a cap advertising some local merchant's wares. He walked with a determined step, his eyes shifting from one spot to another. Minx owned a little farm where he raised his family, grew a garden and fed some chickens and a few head of cattle.

One day he came into my office and asked me to come look at some calves. He said they had the "pneumonia fever." I told him I would be at his place shortly.

A few minutes after Minx left my office I went to his farm. I drove into the barn lot across the road from the house and blew my car horn. No response. I waited a little while and honked the horn again. Finally a tiny lady, who I assumed was Mrs. Salyers, walked across the road. After proper greetings she told me her husband wasn't home yet; he had to go to the feed store after he left my place. Mrs. Salyers and I talked a while and in about ten minutes her husband came driving up the dusty country road in his old black Ford pickup truck. He pulled into the barn lot, stopped behind my car, and grunted a sullen "Hello." Mrs. Salyers said nothing more. She walked back across the road and into the house.

Again I asked Minx about his trouble. He muttered, "These calves is all breathin' hard. One of 'em got real lame and died two days ago." Looking me straight in the eye he said, "Doctor, they got the pneumonia fever." He stopped talking long enough to let his diagnosis soak in on me. During the pause he reached into his bibbed overall front pocket and pulled out a six inch twist of tobacco and with his long thin bladed pocket knife, cut himself a big piece and stuck it in his mouth. He chewed a chomp or two and switching the tobacco to the other cheek, he asked, "What are you goin' to do about it?"

"Minx," I said, taking the liberty of using his calling name and trying to be friendly, "there's a vaccine for pneumonia we can give them if that is what is really wrong, but so far I haven't seen an animal yet. You told me you had a calf that died a day or two ago that was lame. Are you certain that calf had pneumonia?"

"Mister," I know th' pneumonia fever when I see it. You just give 'em the shots." Then he paused and added, "The shots won't kill 'em will it?" I assured him the medicine was safe. Looking me straight in the face he said, "It better not." By this time we had walked into the barn and in a stall were several calves, maybe four or five months old. I took one calf's temperature and it was normal. I felt around on the other's and with my stethoscope listened to their lungs for unusual noises. I checked another calf and the results were the same. At this point these calves were not sick and showed me no indication of lung disease. I talked with Minx and I talked some more about the vaccine, and in return I got some guttural answers. I walked back to my car and got the vaccine and a syringe.

I explained more about the vaccine and told him it was not a sure cure but since most of these calves came from the local stockyard, it would probably help them. I also suggested we could use a combination vaccine that would give protection against Black Leg and Malignant Edema as well as shipping fever, or as he called it, pneumonia fever. He told me he was not interested in anything else.

I injected each calf with the vaccine for shipping fever only. He dug down in his bib overall pocket, dug out a brand new check book and a stub of a pencil. He said, "Mister, you fill 'er out. I can't see too good without my glasses." He saw well enough to make a signature. I backed out of the barn lot and glancing out of the window I saw Mrs. Salyers standing in the door-way, wiping her hands on her apron. I waved good-bye. She showed no sign of response.

I gave a lot of thought to the Salyers and their ways but they were no different than the other hill people. They were reluctant to face a changing world and maybe they weren't so sure about me, a new young doctor, or what I was doing. I drove back to my office and soon forgot about the Salyers and their calves.

Three or four nights later, the State Police called me and let me know that Mr. Minx Salyers wanted me at his farm as soon as I could get there. I thanked the dispatcher for the call but before he hung up he said, "Doc, that man seems pretty mad."

It was a cold fall night and the rain was pouring down when I pulled into the barn lot. Minx was standing in the doorway of the barn waiting for me. A kerosene lantern, hanging on a nail, cast a pale yellow light in the dark barn. In the dim light I couldn't help from seeing a rifle leaning against the door frame. I got out of my car and summoning all of the bravado I could, I said hello and asked what was wrong. About that time two younger men came from the behind the barn, apparently Minx's sons. The older one was dressed like his daddy, right down to the knee high rubber boots. The other man had a short beard and walked a little stooped over like he'd carried too many heavy bales of hay or sacks full of cow feed. He was hunkered down inside his rust colored Carharrt coat, trying to stay warm. They never said a word—they just stood there in the pouring down rain staring at me. In the meantime, I was getting cold and wet and I stepped past Minx into the log barn out of the rain.

Before I could say a word Minx started on me. "Your shots killed one of my calves. Now what are you going to do about that?"

I had never been in a situation like this before, and I nervously wondered what what he was going to do. The man with the beard stepped past me into the barn out of the cold rain. I asked him what they had done with the calf. Before he could answer, the other man, still outside in the rain said, "We done drug it up over the hill to the woods."

"Let's us go look at it. I'll take my post-mortem knife and we'll find out what killed the calf. Still apprehensive as I could be, I forced my point and told Minx, "The vaccine didn't hurt your calves. Something else caused the animal to die."

The four us climbed the hill, slipping and sliding in the mud, Minx leading the way, carrying the lantern in one hand, the rifle in the other. I was second in line and the two Salyers boys followed after me. We must have walked about two hundred yards when we came to a barbed wire fence. The younger man growled, "The calf's across the fence in a ditch." I crawled through the fence and followed Minx and his lantern over to the dead calf. The yellow lantern light, sputtering in the heavy rain, reflected off Minx's face, giving him a ghoulish appearance. In the distance a dog howled, was quiet a minute, and then gave another even longer howl.

I had to keep my composure, be professional and, by all means, be forceful or at least act like I was in command. I must admit, I was frightened. I had never been faced with a gun before except in the war and that was different. By the time we got to the dead calf, I had it all figured out. I knew what I was going to do.

"Mr. Salyers, you hold the lantern over here so I can see." I watched him as he handed the gun to one of his boys. I stooped down and ran my hands over the dead calf and as I felt along the heavy muscles of his hips and loin, I could feel the familiar crepitation where the black leg bacteria had created gas under the animal's skin. Now I was absolutely in control and had a firm diagnosis in my mind. All I had to do now was convince Minx. "Mr. Salyers, you are a smart man." I hoped my psychology would work. "You told me you knew what the pneumonia fever looked like. If you'll remember I talked to you about the lame-calf, the one that died, and suggested it might have black leg. You also told me you knew what that disease looked like." Before he could answer, I jabbed the long blade of the post-mortem knife into the swollen leg and in the light of the sputtering lantern and the discomfort of the pouring down rain revealed the blackened, bloody, swollen tissue of a typical case of the disease.

Minx Salyers mellowed as best he could and said, "By God, young man, you're right. Let's go get out of this weather." The hound bayed again, a long soulful howl, this time it was a little closer.

One of the brothers, the one holding the rifle, turned to Minx and said, "Pap, you and the doctor can handle this. Brother and me'll go and shoot that coon that old dog has got treed."

Way out on the ridge, in spite of the constant noise of the falling rain, the dog howled again, this time the sweetest sound I ever heard. That gun was for a racoon, not me.

§   §   §

It was getting colder, and two days before Thanksgiving, Mary Helen took Terri and went to Portsmouth for the holiday and the traditional family feast. I promised I would drive down Wednesday night after office hours. This would work out fine and the grandparents would have plenty of time to ooh and ah over Baby Terri.

Just before my office hours were over, the phone rang and a man who said he was Windy Roach told me he had some real sick calves. Would I come look at them? They were good veal calves and worth, according to him, "considerable money." I assured him I would come after I closed my office, while assuring myself there would be a considerable fee! He told me he lived the first house on the left after you passed the Grange Hall in Deering, Ohio. I knew exactly where it was. I called long distance to Mary Helen in Portsmouth and told her I would be late.

At the first house past the Deering Grange Hall, I turned into the drive and, in my customary way, sounded the car horn announcing my arrival. At the same time I turned up the heat control in my car to stay warm while I waited for Mr. Roach. Impatiently I blew the car horn again; a light came on at the back porch door and Roach, shouting from the porch, told me he had a long distance phone caller on the line. "If you don't mind," he said with a slight lisp, "I'll be with you as soon as I get off the phone." At the same time he pointed to a path that headed toward the barn. To save time I buttoned up my heavy coat, picked up my medical bag and a flashlight and started down the path to the barn.

I hadn't gone too far when I heard something rustling in the weeds beside me. I stopped, shined my light in the direction of the noise but saw nothing. I took three of four more steps and heard the noises again all around me. I was a little apprehensive. Two or three steps later Roach caught up with me and apologized for the delay and stepped in front of me to lead me to the barn. I didn't mention the strange noises. When Windy opened the door and turned on the electric lights, in absolute shock I looked at about fifteen or twenty calves and literally hundreds of great big rats. Rats were all over the place, some standing on their hind feet fighting other rats! Laying in a corner of the barn were two dead calves. Rats were swarming all over them. Now I realized what was making the noise outside and suddenly I wasn't cold anymore. I was drenched in sweat from fright! When the lights came on the rats disappeared and I stood there dumbfounded, with some sick and dead veal calves and Mr. Roach.

After I examined some of the calves and looked over the whole situation, I suggested we go back to my warm car away from the rat-infested building and discuss the case. As we closed the car doors and the warm heat from the heater did its work, I talked to Roach and diagnosed his problem as leptospirosis, a disease harbored by rodents and transmittable to people. I suggested to my client he see his physician and terminate his calf operation. He did both, and by an act of fate, the barn burned down a few weeks later sterilizing the ground.

I drove on to Portsmouth, had a good Turkey Day and a visit with both families. Later on Thanksgiving afternoon it started to snow and, since Mary Helen and the baby planned to stay over the weekend, I drove back to Kentucky. That was the winter of 1950 and the blizzard that made history. I got home OK but it took ten days before the snows were cleared away enough for my family to get back to Ashland.

We celebrated our first Christmas in our new home and one evening after I was through working, Mary Helen and I recapped the first six months of our new lifestyle and the practice. It had been an eye-opening period of time, mixed with the usual and the unusual. Finally, as if trying to sum up our conversation, my pretty wife looked me straight in the eye said, "You know, honey, the way things have turned out, I don't think we will ever have a ho-hum day."

How right that was.

Not Much Time for Settin' and Rockin'

SUMMER AND FALL WERE GOOD MONTHS FOR BUSINESS AND JUST PLAIN living. It was a good time—if you ever had the time—as one old timer up a 'holler' told me, ". . . to jest set and rock" and enjoy the pretty weather. That was fine as long as you didn't have to work and as long as the weather was fair. It stays decent weather here in Kentucky 'til about Thanksgiving, then it gets cold and you can expect snow just about anytime. The big snows don't generally come until after Christmas. January and February are the worst months, with March throwing a surprise spring storm once in a while. This was another good time to "set and rock," time to enjoy the fireplace on those cold winter days. But I was like the mailman, I had to make my rounds in spite of the weather, delivering my veterinary services, healing the animals and consoling their owners. As a general rule, Kentucky weather is not too extreme; our winters were not too cold and not too snowy. When it did snow, it didn't take it long to melt away. But every once in a while the almanac predictions were wrong and then it was winter for certain.

§ § §

The first winter we were in Kentucky was an exception. The big snow paralyzed everything and I made the best of it. I had to; I had a family to support and bills to pay. Discomforts of my job also magnified when I had calls to make—the business slowed to a crawl simply because it was too

49

nasty to get out. Getting stuck in snow drifts and on muddy roads was not uncommon. The other discomforts of my job also were magnified as the weather worsened. My clients, their farm work done for the season, were content to be at home. Their firewood was cut and stacked, the gardens were finished except for a few turnips to be pulled, and for all practical reasons, the small farms were dormant. Only the dairy farmer worked at full speed the year around. My cold job, however, was made more tolerable by the warmth of the people. I really think some of my farm calls seemed like social visits to my isolated country clients.

On Monday morning, the winter of '51, I had two calls to make, both at Bear Creek, a good farming section about fifteen miles south of town. It was an absolutely nasty, bitter cold day. While I checked my medical bag with what I thought I would need, outside my office I could hear the wind howl as it drove blinding gusts of snow and ice against the building. I glanced through the window at a thermometer I had put up outside a few weeks earlier and it read a cold fifteen degrees above zero! The windchill factor must have been below zero. It was just an awful day to be outside. The main highway would be passable, but I wasn't sure about the county gravel roads.

I bundled up in my heavy winter coat, turned the car heater all the way up to "hot" and started toward my first visit to look at some young hogs that were sick. The gusting, swirling snow flurries, besieging the car in spite of the fact the windshield wipers were going at top speed, made it almost impossible for me to see. I pushed on through the snow drifts, skidding and sliding, slowly making my way along the Bear Creek Road. Suddenly my car broke through the ice into a deep mud hole and came to a jarring stop! It was stuck. I shifted from one gear to another, backwards and forwards, but nothing helped. There was no choice but to try to find some help. The Hardin farm was about a half a mile away. I knew they would help me or at least keep me warm until we could get assistance.

I got out of my nice warm car, pulled the ear flaps down on my winter hat, huddled down in my heavy winter coat and waded through the deep snow to the house. I knocked on the door. No one answered. I knew someone had to be there because there wasn't a track out of the driveway. I knocked the second time and, after what seemed like an eternity, Mrs. Hardin opened the door and stood there for just a second, hardly believing what must have seemed like an apparition coming at her out of the swirling snow. She hustled me into the kitchen, pointed to the big, hot, coal stove in one corner of the room and at the same time poured me a cup of steaming coffee. "Get yourself warm and drink this, Doctor Martin," she said. "I'll call Lace from the barn." Lace was her grown son and sure enough after she called him from the back door he came into the house, stomping the snow off of his boots as he came into his mother's kitchen. I told him what happened as he reached for the cup of hot coffee his mother poured for him.

"Now, Doc," Lace said with his ever pleasant grin, "just warm yourself and I'll go get the mules. We'll get you out of that hole in no time." He set his coffee cup down and, pulling his coat collar up around his face, turned and walked out the door toward the barn. I finished the coffee. It went through my mind that I could just stay there all day enjoying the warmth and my friends.

Lace was back at the house in a matter of a few minutes with his team of big sorrel mules. He motioned me outside, handed me the bridle reigns of one of the mules and said, "Doc, you ride Barney and I'll straddle Sam here and we'll go get your car." Together we rode mule-back through my foot tracks in the snow the long half mile to my car. Lace hooked the tow chain to my car, the other end to the mules' harness and with my help with the motor, Sam and Barney did their job and pulled me out of that hole. Satisfied I was OK, Lace unhooked his team and headed for the house. I followed in the car. I offered to pay for the mule service, but Lace and his mother both refused to take any money. Lace said, "Now, Doc, takin' your money for that just ain't our way. It just wouldn't be neighborly." He went on, "But I do want to show you somethin'. Put your coat back on and go to the barn with me—I'll show you my colts." I followed him out the door and we walked out the path to the big stock barn about fifty yards from the house.

Inside that big barn, on the left side of the hallway, were four big roomy box stalls. Lace had Barney in one and Sam in another. In the stalls next to the mules were two fat, slick young horses, one a chestnut, the other a sorrel with a blazed face—Lace's pride and joy. I no sooner walked up to the stall to look at the first horse when all hell broke loose. The horse lunged at me with his mouth open, snapping like a mad dog and striking at me with his hooves. I was the enemy; the horse intended to destroy me! Only the heavy oak boards of the stall protected me. I jumped back and Lace laughed so hard I thought his face would burst from redness. Clouds of frozen steam from his breath filled the barn alley while he told me that his colts were both three years old. He said, "Doc, they ain't never as much as had a halter on 'em." They were simply wild animals, used to Lace but seeing me as a complete stranger—an invader. I asked him where he bought them. He exploded,"Bought 'em Hell, I raised 'em from two old mares we have here at the farm."

"How do you expect to break these wild stallions?"

"Doc Martin, they won't be no problem at all after you change 'em, come next spring."

Later that spring when the dogwood was in bloom and the redbud trees made the hills look pretty, I did indeed "change" those colts but I worried the rest of the winter how I was going to do it. It turned out they were really not a big problem after I got my lasso rope on them, and after some ingenuity and tricky effort, gave them an intravenous injection that put them to sleep. But that was later when the cold left.

I repeated my sincere thanks to the Hardins and, warm from their hospitality and hot coffee, I went on my way to look at the sick pigs on a farm about five miles on down the creek.

Squatting down in the hog pen, inside the dark barn with just my flashlight for help, I examined the pigs. They had a disease that made them lame and caused diamond-shaped skin lesions over most of their bodies. I treated the sick animals and explained the consequences of this disease, erysipelas, to Mr. Quesenberry, the owner. Just as I started to stand up, one of the bigger pigs bumped me and I tumbled backwards. As soon as I hit the ground, I got the shock of my life. I had fallen on an electric wire Quesenberry had hooked to a fence charger to keep the pigs from rooting their way to freedom. I got up, nothing but my dignity hurt, and after a chuckle or two, said my goodbye to the pig owner and once again drove away in a blinding snow storm.

Two miles later the Bear Creek Road ended at a paved highway. The snow plow had done its job, and as long as I stayed on that road, I had no trouble. But this didn't last long, and in just a few minutes I had to turn off the paved road to Bob Bloebaum's place to treat a sick cow. This animal had calved three days earlier and had not passed her placenta. Solving that problem was a common veterinary medical challange everybody referred to as, "cleaning a cow."

I finally got to the lane that turned off the county road and started toward Bloebaum's. The house was about three hundred yards up a hollow from the road; I shifted into low gear and started up the narrow lane, going very slow to be sure I didn't slide off into the ditch. Suddenly my car jarred to a stop—I was stuck again! Once again I bundled up my coat, got my medical bag and walked on toward the warm farmhouse.

By now it was almost dark, way past my usual supper time, and I was hungry, as well as frustrated over the snow and its consequences. The light at the end of the road got closer, and as I started thinking about the Hardin hospitality, I thought maybe I could get warm this time at the Bloebaum's. And then I smelled the aroma coming from the kitchen. I didn't know when I ever smelled food like this and it just increased my gnawing hunger!

Mr. Bloembaum met me at the door, and never hesitating he said, "Doc, take off your coat and warm up by the fire. My wife says supper will be ready in just a few minutes."

Mrs. B. came into the living room and wiping her hands on her apron, she apologized for her scanty meal, "Doctor, it's just cat head biscuits and homemade vegetable soup."

Now I have been all over the world and have eaten in some fancy places, but never did I have food as good as those biscuits and vegetable soup. I'm afraid I overdid because I asked for and did get second helpings!

I finished my supper, tended the cow and started back home. The beams of my headlights cut holes in the dark and I could see it had stopped snowing. The clouds were breaking and the moon shone down on the white snow, lighting up the hill country like magic. I drove the few miles home and now that my day was over, I was so proud to be part of a community that had such nice people with their caring ways.

§ § §

Two years later we had another bad winter with a lot of snow and bitter cold temperatures. This winter spawned some unusual happenings too. My practice by now had grown considerably, and it was not uncommon to travel long distances to tend my sick patients. Late one evening Booten Hall, a nice farmer in Greenup County (the county just west of where we lived), called and asked me to come deliver a calf from a heifer he owned. Before I could say, "Yes, I'll come," he told me the young cow was in an old tobacco barn on top of a hill, two or three hundred yards from the road. Booten said he would meet me at the covered bridge over Tygart Creek down at Kehoe, a small community that consisted of a post office and three or four houses.

It was close to thirty miles to our meeting place, and when I got there Hall was waiting. He got out of his pickup truck and into my warm car and told me to drive up the road to his pasture. "Stop here." I did. He opened the gate and told me this was as far as we could go. We had to walk from there up the hill to the cow.

I gathered my obstetrical instruments and everything else I thought I needed. Numb with the cold I followed Mr. Hall up the hill, every step an effort. The deep snow and the extreme cold were about all I could take. Then I got to thinking, if Mr. Hall, who was about fifty, could make it up this hill, then so could I with my twenty-eight years strength. I shrugged deeper into my coat and walked on to the top of the hill.

We found the cow inside the old tobacco barn as described, but the ancient building was in the process of being torn down. Most of the roof was gone and what was left of the sides was far from a wind break. The wind carried blowing snow and ice crystals through the cracks in the walls with every gust.

I stuck my flashlight in a crack in the barn wall to direct some light on the heifer. It was obvious she had been bred too young and could not deliver without help. By the time we got there, she had presented the calf part way and the pressure it put on the nerves that lined her pelvis caused her to be paralyzed—she couldn't stand up. I muttered to Hall it would sure be nice if we had some hot water so we could wash the mud and the filth off of my patient. Hall answered back, as he pulled his coat closer to his face , "Doctor, hot water is out of the question." He hesitated a minute and added, "There is an old well back here but that won't help us. Its bound to be froze over."

During this conversation I had removed my coat and shirt and down on my knees I did a preliminary examination. When Hall mentioned the well, I struggled back to my feet and, as I got up, pulled my coat back over my bare shoulder and arm that was wet from the fluids and filth of the cow.

Looking around I found a wrecking bar hanging on the partially torn down wall. Picking it up I suggested to Mr. Hall we try and pry some of the old building foundation stones from under the building and drop them down the well and break the ice. If this worked, we could lower my bucket with my lasso rope and get some water. We used the wrecking bar and finally managed to pry three big rocks from the frozen ground. I dropped the largest stone down in the well. The ice cracked. Then we dropped the second big stone and, glory be, it broke through and we had water. I managed to clean up the cow as best I could with some towels and the ice water. Then Hall and I together delivered a dead calf. I saved enough water to wash with when I was done but when I did, that ice water was like sticking knives into my bare hands and arms. Once more the thoughts went through my mind that there had to be a better way to make a living—but I knew there wasn't, at least for me!

We packed all of the equipment and stumbled through the snow down the hill to the warm car. Booten Hall was grateful I had made such an effort, in spite of losing the calf. As it turned out, the cow died too from the extreme cold and stress of an impossible birth. Mr. Hall was a good client for many years and every time I saw him, he would chuckle and never fail to ask if I had taken any more baths in ice cold well water.

§   §   §

Just three nights later Reverend Henry, a minister at the Pentecostal Church out on Indian Run Road, called me. He was frantic. "Mister, my cow's done had a nice big calf but now she can't stand up. She's a dyin', I know it! Please, sir, come rat now!" I assured him I would be "rat" there—rat meaning in hill talk, right—and for him to have some hot water and towels ready when I got there. He promised he would. I had no trouble finding the place on Indian Run with his good directions.

We were still in the grips of the bitter winter weather: the thermometer this night read an even zero! The storm was over, and as the cold front passed through, the sky was as clear as a bell. Every star winked its brightest, each trying to outdo the other. But along with the stars, there was a weird light in the sky, dancing from the horizon along the hills, fading out and then flaring high into the heavens. It was the Aurora Borealis—the Northern Lights.

I had seen this phenomenon only twice before, but I knew what I was seeing and was fascinated by it. My client, a man of the cloth, was just plain scared! He made no bones about being uneasy, even after I assured him that the light was one of God's ways with the weather and we were OK.

As we walked out to his little barn, it was so cold the snow squeaked under your feet. Once in the barn, I diagnosed the cow as having milk fever, a condition of improper mineral balance usually associated with heavy milk producing cows. I took my bottle of medicine from under my warm coat and injected it into the cow's blood stream. Most of these patients respond rapidly, and this one was no different, getting well in front of the owner's eyes. At this rapid response, my man-of-the-cloth vowed that I had done some magic!

I finished treating my patient and assured preacher Henry she would be all right. Finally we went to his house for both of us to get warm and for me to get my money. First thing Henry said was, "Mister,"—during the entire visit I was never honored with my title as a doctor—"God bless you for hepin' me." He paused and looked out the kitchen window and the Aurora blazed again, this time brighter than ever. His face ashen white from uncertainty, he turned back to me and said, "I'm a thankin' you again on this strange night of the Lord." And then as an afterthought he added, "Remember I am just a poor Pentecostal preacher, so don't charge me too much!"

On this cold night I found little humor, just amazement, in his remark. But then it seems like a thing people often say, if they are poor ministers. I was learning a lot about people. Most were appreciative, some more self-serving. I added five dollars to the normal fee and when I got home I told Mary Helen to put the extra cash in her church donation the next Sunday. She smiled and did just that.

§   §   §

We survived the physical discomforts of the winter and even though these hardships played a major role in the practice, the biggest hardship was the money—paying the bills.

When we first came to Ashland we had very little money, but we had friends and the determination to make it work. Thanks to Henri Riekert and the rest of the people in Boyd County, we established a practice. But with the good practice there were business hardships too. I never let it get me down and I was never late paying a bill. When the statements came in the mail, and it was bill-paying time, we took the oldest one and put it on top of the pile and paid it first. Somehow we managed. In a few years we had a sustaining practice. Still we never got rich in spite of what some people thought. It always irked me when some one would say "Doc, if we had your money . . . " I had a fast answer to them—if they put in the hours a day I did, they would have more cash than Doc Martin.

There was very little time for settin' and rockin' in our lifestyle.

PART OF GOD'S PLAN

THE WINTER SNOWS FINALLY MELTED AND THE WEAK RAYS OF AN EARLY spring sunshine warmed the steps of our house as I sat sipping my breakfast coffee. I watched the last of the morning fog burn away and uncover the hills, their trees still bare of leaves from their long winter sleep. It was a beautiful Sunday morning and I looked forward to what the day would bring.

My thoughts were interrupted by the telephone, the life blood of my embryonic veterinary practice. The state police barracks, in spite of a slowly expanding rural telephone system, was still my phone relay station. The dispatcher told me Mrs. Preece's horse stepped into a hole and she thought the leg was broken. The officer also said the lady told him, "I would sure appreciate it if the doctor will come as quick as he can."

I drove the twenty miles to the Preece farm and treated the injured horse. The leg was badly bruised, but not broken. When I finished my work Mrs. Preece invited me into her kitchen for a cup of coffee and to question me about caring for her animal. She was pleased when I told her the prognosis was good and I expected a complete recovery. As she handed me my coffee cup, she turned her head toward the living room and called to her daughter, "Sharon, fetch the money for the Doctor." In less than a minute a very pretty and a very pregnant young lady handed her mother some money and left the room. The mother, chuckling and pointing to her daughter said, "You know, Doctor, spring is birthing time for everything here in Kentucky." That was the first time I ever heard it put that way, but it seemed to fit.

Kentucky springtime with its burst of fresh new color, brings the rebirth of the woods, the rivers and the hills. The land becomes alive after hibernating through those long cold winter months. It is also birthing time for most of the animals, and sometimes—humankind too!

59

Most of the veterinary birthing cases involve cattle, but all of the animals at times need help delivering their young. The small lambs we see in the pasture fields frequently have problems just getting into our world, their mothers suffering hard labor and, I am sure, severe pain. Mares are no exception and in rare instances need help to deliver their foals. Likewise, sows often have difficulty farrowing, especially if they are gilts. Gilts are the young sows, bred for the first time. Veterinarians are well trained in obstetrical procedures and our services are in great demand during the spring of the year.

§   §   §

About a week after I treated the horse with the injured leg, I had another call from the police dispatcher. The officer told me that a lady by the name of Riffe, in Lawrence County, had a sow trying to have pigs. She needed my help. The policeman also filled me in on the rest of the story. "Doc Martin, she told me when Mr. Riffe got in his old pickup truck and started to the county seat to call you, he hadn't gone a mile when his truck skidded in the mud and came to rest in the ditch. He got stuck good and couldn't get any farther."

I knew this was going to be a good story so I asked officer Charles, whom I knew as a friend, "What else did she say?"

"Well, Doctor, she went on to tell me a neighbor came along and promised he would stop in here and give us the message. She said the neighbor was goin' to a church meeting in Ashland, and since our office was on the way, it wouldn't be neighborly if he didn't help."

I asked Charles how to get to the Riffe place. And after giving me exact directions, he added as an afterthought that it was in a very remote part of the county. "It's on a long ridge road just before you get to Blaine Town up in the big hill country. The road ain't all bad but it twists and turns like a snake." Mary Helen and Terri, now five years old, sometimes went on calls with me and since this was a beautiful spring morning, they were ready to go.

I drove the thirty miles of twisting Kentucky roads, the last two, just as Charles the dispatcher said, along the top of a high ridge until I came to a mailbox crudely lettered with the name "Riffe." We could see the house down in a little hollow about a hundred yards below the graveled road. I got out of my car, picked up my medical bag and started down the steep path, Terri right on my heels. Mary Helen said she was content to stay in the car and read her book. Half way down the steep uncertain path a woman climbed the hill to meet us. As she came closer she said, holding out her hand for a friendly shake, "You must be th' hog doctor. I'm th' missus." She hesitated and then added, "Mrs. Riffe." I smiled and shook her hand.

Mrs. Riffe appeared to be on the young side of middle age, thin and weathered from the hardships of raising her family in the mountains of our land. Her hair, fastened in a bun, was streaked with gray—a few strands falling down her thin, wind-burned cheeks. She wore a long, faded blue dress that reached nearly to her ankles. Over that she had on a homemade apron fashioned from flour sacks that had been scrubbed and scrubbed until the word "Pillsbury" was barely visible. Her only sign of vanity was a large blue calico pocket sewed to the apron. It appeared to hold most of her personal belongings. Her outward appearance was misleading. She was, in reality, a forceful woman, obviously the queen of her domain.

After addressing me, Mrs. Riffe turned to Terri and looking down at my little girl, said, "Honey, you can call me Granny." And then looking up at me and with sincerity she said, "Doctor, you sure got a pretty kid." With that, she turned and started up the path to the top of the hill. "I'll go to th' car and get your missus—then us women folk can go to th' house for a visit."

I was about to tell her that Mary Helen had elected to stay in the car but the lady was already three or four steps up the steep path toward the car and turning her head toward me so I could hear, she said, "Doc, th' old sow's in tha hog lot. My man Orville will hep ya." She turned back towards the house and yelled in a booming voice, "Orville, here's th' hog doctor—hep him." Her colloquialisms were straight from the hills!

Terri and I went to the hog lot to look at the sow while Granny tried to persuade my wife to come down to the house the Riffes called home. We found the sow in a typical filthy, smelly pig pen. She was covered with mud and the first flies of spring were swarming all over her. Up to this point she had produced no piglets but was in a lot of pain and laboring hard.

A reluctant Orville finally made his appearance at the hog lot. He was tall, thin and gaunt and, like Granny, his appearance reflected the rigors and life of the mountain people. He was completely bald headed, and to chase away the chills of the spring from his naked head, he wore an old, faded, red baseball cap. He walked with a slight stoop as if like his bones ached from arthritis brought on by hard work and the difficulty of living in the hill country. Threadbare, faded denim overalls covering a long- sleeved winter undershirt, clean but worn and gray from years of use and rough scrubbing, completed his attire. His presence was not nearly as forceful as his wife's.

Orville just stood there, saying nothing and not too willing to volunteer any help. "Orville," I said, "Let's get this sow out of this filthy pen and clean her up." Adding, "How about to that grassy spot out by that old fence post at the corner of the barn? I'll put this hog-catcher around her nose and pull and at the same time you kinda grab her tail and steer her that way." It worked, in spite of her squealing and struggling, and we got her to the fence post and fastened her to the post with the rope that was looped through her mouth and around her nose.

Orville was persuaded to find some soap, water and clean rags. Together we scrubbed the squealing, squirming mother-to-be so she would be clean enough to work with. By chance I looked toward the cabin and there was my wife standing in the doorway. Granny had insisted she come to the house. Mary Helen stood there and watched as Mrs. Riffe walked toward the hog lot to talk to me.

"Doctor, if pleases ya, I'll take the little girl to tha house. A woman shouldn't be around things like this. Your missus is already over there and we're goin' to visit."

Terri immediately said, "No," insisting she had to help her daddy. She was not quite six years old when this happened and was convinced I couldn't practice without her. I sided with my daughter and a frowning, muttering Granny made her way back to the house.

I examined the sow who was trying to have her first litter and immediately determined her pelvis was too small for her to have a normal delivery. A Caesarean operation would be needed. I looked up from my job, washed my hands and went to the house to tell Mrs. Riffe what I was going to do.

The Riffe house was no different than many others that dotted our rural landscape. Like most mountain houses it had started as a one-room log cabin. As time progressed and the families increased in size, more rooms were added and eventually siding of some sort was nailed over the logs. Granny's house had two rooms, a porch across the front and a cistern for water in the front yard. Out the back door a path led to a privy that looked like it would fall down any minute. The barn and the hog pen, by comparison, were in far better shape.

Mrs. Riffe met me at the door and as we talked, I looked over her shoulder into the cabin at about ten children, stair-stepped in size, all staring first at me and then back at Mary Helen. I managed to explain what I had to do and, after she gave me the Lord's Blessing, hesitantly she told me that surely all of her troubles had to be part of God's Plan. I wasn't sure just what she meant by that statement but it was plainly evident the Riffes were God-fearing people.

I went back to the hog lot and my job. Orville was no place to be seen. It was pretty obvious that he didn't relish the idea of watching me operate. That was no problem, since I had my fine, nearly six-year-old assistant. I didn't need his help.

I put my surgical instruments in a bucket full of clean water and added some disinfectant. Then I got a bottle of anesthetic medicine out of my black bag and filled my syringe. Slowly, I injected the medicine into a vein in the sow's ear and in a minute or two, she was sound asleep. I managed with Terri's help to roll the sow over on her back and tie her in that position with my ropes. Together, daughter and I scrubbed the sow's belly and painted it with iodine. At this point, my daughter, with more iodine on her than on the pig, was in her glory.

Terri, sitting beside the sow's head with her knees propped under her chin, watched as I performed the surgery. As I worked I kept wondering about Granny's remarks that all of this was part of God's Plan. As the surgery progressed, I eventually delivered six wet, squirming baby pigs and one by one, handed then to my daughter. She tried her best to wipe each piglet clean with a dry rag and when she was satisfied they were dry, she put them in an old basket we found in the barn. Then, working as fast as I could, I closed the surgical wounds, untied the sow and gave her a shot of penicillin while she was still asleep. The operation was a complete success and the sow, now blinking her eyes, was out of danger and was slowly waking up.

Finished, I looked up and there came Orville. He stopped, stared first at the sleeping sow then at me. He took off his faded baseball cap and wiped the sweat away from his bald head on his shirt sleeve. Putting the cap back on with a tug and looking at my sleeping patient, the first thing he asked me was, "Is she dead?" I assured him she was not. The second thing he wanted to do, now convinced she was still alive, was put her back in the muddy lot. He said, "I reckon she'll heal better in the mud." I reckoned she would be better off in the clean grassy place where I operated on her. I won and she stayed—at least while I was there.

Terri and I washed and packed my surgical instruments and medicine into my black bag. We walked to the farmhouse and I explained to a pleased Granny Riffe what I had done. I told her she had six new baby pigs and explained how to care for them. Once again I received the Lord's Blessings and thanks. Then she said, "Iff'n you'll set a spell, I'll fix us some dinner." Looking at that swarm of kids and the drama of the Riffe family, we tactfully backed out of that offer. Just before we were ready to go, Granny sat down on the edge of the porch and from the big blue calico pocket in her apron pulled out some tobacco and cigarette papers and deftly rolled a cigarette. She lit it with a big wooden match, and with a deep drag, inhaled the smoke. Terri was fascinated by all of this and gawked at this old lady in disbelief. Finally, with a twinkle in her eye, Granny asked her if she had ever seen anyone roll a smoke before. My daughter didn't answer, just continued to stare in amazement.

We said our goodbyes and climbed the steep path up the hill to our car. As we were ready to leave, we waved and I saw Orville standing out by the old barn. With very little enthusiasm, he waved back. He seemed to be deep in thought.

Mary Helen had enjoyed her visit with this hill woman and that story has to be told too.

To begin with, an eastern Kentucky rural electric company had just recently run electricity to the area and with the passing of the kerosene lamps not only came lights but radio and the new marvel of television as well. The oldest Riffe boy was away in the Marines and when electric power came to Granny's, so did a new TV from her Marine Corps son. Orville bought a radio, and Granny had them both going at once, and all of the time Mary Helen was in her parlor, blaring the Sunday morning gospel, directly from more than one house of the Lord.

Granny, chattering away, told Mary Helen about their recent bad luck. She started her story by asking, "Mrs. Martin, do you think th' good Lord is punishin' us for havin' this television machine the boy give us? Seems like we've had nothin' but troubles ever since it come." Mary Helen avoided asking her for the details. "Now my sow's sick and this mornin' th' mister," another mountain colloquialism, "wrecked his truck when he went to fetch Doc Martin." And then, changing to another topic she mentioned something else, ". . . then them tax people come here too." M.H. did not pursue that story!

My wife consoled her and assured her that the Lord was not trying to punish them because even some preachers had television sets and radios. She said she didn't know anything about, ". . . the tax business." I think my wife made her point.

The drive back home was beautiful. Warm spring weather had filled the Kentucky hills with white dogwood blossoms. Scattered among them, as an added attraction, the redbud trees were in full bloom. About a half a mile out the ridge and around a curve, where the view was absolutely breathtaking, I stopped the car and we took in the view. At one side of the road we saw jonquils, their yellow blooms standing tall in a little flat area where an old farmhouse once stood. Toads in the mud holes along the road filled the air with their music. Far down in the hollow we saw the Riffe place, and out by the barn I made out Orville. I'm sure he thought we were gone and out of sight. He was dragging the still sleepy sow and the old basket full of her babies toward the healing mud hole! Starting the car we drove on. The clean mountain air smelled good, and driving along the rough road, I mused that the sow would soon be suckling her babies and with a little attention from Granny would be fine. My thoughts continued, now about Granny. Hopefully she was more at ease about her television and was convinced, with Mary Helen's assurance, that she wasn't a sinner. It had been a good trip and Granny Riffe was right—it all had to be part of God's Plan.

§   §   §

The Reverend Ed Owney owned two large farms about twenty miles south of town, back toward the big hill country. The working part of his holdings was on Bolt's Fork. Over seven hundred acres of woods and pasture land was not far away, but over in a section the locals called Seed Tick. Reverend Owney was a fine, compassionate man, a practicing minister and, to my knowledge, didn't have an enemy in the world. He lived in town, but when he was not actively serving his congregation, you could always find him at one farm or the other. He was a very good farmer and knew how to make a dollar.

He came into the office early one morning and, while he watched me sew up a cut on a dog's leg, told me he had a small Hereford heifer in hard labor. "Doctor, we have not as much as touched her. Tony found her in the lower pasture and drove her to the barn." Tony Arnett was Ed's hired man and also a very nice person. "We will be waiting for you. I would feel kindly if you can work me in your schedule." I appreciated his courtesy and promised him I would be there as soon as I finished my minor dog surgery. In a few minutes I put in my last stitch and was done. I drove straight to the Owney farm on Bolt's Fork.

Ed and Tony were waiting for me and thoughtfully made some arrangements. Set in the doorway to the harness room was a five gallon lard can full of steaming hot water. A cardboard box full of clean rags and a bar of Ivory soap was beside the can. The heifer, straining hard in her labor, was in the hallway of the barn tied to a post. Seeing these considerate arrangements, the thought went through my mind how nice my life would be if all of my clients were as efficient and thoughtful.

I examined the cow and found in the straining process the calf's head had been forced back along the side of its body. It was also very evident that the heifer's pelvic canal was too small for a normal delivery. I managed to get an obstetrical chain around the calf's head and straighten it, so it lay on top of the forelegs in a normal birthing position. In addition to the head chain, I placed a chain around each of the calf's front legs, just above its tiny hooves.

"Ed," I said, taking liberty with his holy title, "You and Tony take hold of these chain handles and when I tell you to pull, you do it with a strong and steady pull. Just don't jerk. Also, when I tell you to stop, do it right away. Understand?" He said they understood.

So we started. I began with a quart of mineral oil for lubrication, put my gloved arm into the heifer and told them to pull on the chains. Nothing happened. They pulled again, this time harder. Nothing happened this time either. I remembered one time my obstetrics teacher in college telling us, " . . . if you can't deliver a calf with muscles alone, you better think of another way." I activated my new plan which was to replace Reverend Owney and his hired man, Tony, with the obstetrical block and tackle. We went through the same procedure, Tony pulling the ropes of the come-along but the results were the same—nothing happened! It was evident we couldn't deliver the calf this way either and to avoid hurting this young mother-to-be, I removed the chains and had a talk with Reverend Ed.

"Ed, I can't deliver this calf this way and if we are going to save the cow, and maybe the calf, I believe the only answer is a Caesarean section operation."

"Dr. Martin," he was more particular with my title than I had been with his, "you are the boss. Tells us what to do."

With these consoling words, and not telling I had never done one on a cow, I laid out my plans, gave them their instructions, and we began the job.

I had Tony get a scrub brush and with some soap and water he scrubbed the heifer's left flank until he nearly had the hair scrubbed off! When he was finished, I lathered her up with some more soap and with a razor that was in my surgical kit shaved away the hair over a large section of her left flank. Once again I had him scrub the cow and when he was finished, the young cow was far cleaner than Tony. (I was quite sure he didn't use this much soap and water in a week).

I painted the operation site with iodine, infiltrated the skin and under-tissues with novocaine. I also injected a local anesthetic into the spinal cord just forward of her tail. This stopped her straining but made her legs weak and she lay down. This was fine with me. In lieu of surgical drapes I covered the operation site with newspapers that, at my request, Tony brought from his house. I had Ed and Tony wash their hands, and after I put on my surgical gloves, I started the operation.

I made a big bold incision through the flank, on down through the muscle layers through the shiny peritoneum—the slick tissue that lines the body cavity. This exposed the bulging, calf-filled uterus. Already I was patting myself on the back—hopefully brother Ed and helper Tony were impressed.

All this time I was sitting on my heels, everything going just like I had seen it in college, only lacking the clean surgery suite, bright surgery lights, surgically-draped patients and properly suited students and helpers. Carefully I packed some sterile sponges around the edges of the wound and, with my sharp scalpel, and silent prayers, opened the uterus over what I thought were two rear feet. I was right. Hastily I reached into the lard can, now full of disinfectant and surgical instruments, and got the obstetrical chains. As the feet appeared, I fastened the chains just above the tiny hooves. When they were secure, I told Tony to carefully pull the calf out. The calf was alive and Tony was its nurse maid. Ed was elated and watched with fascination as I sutured the uterus closed and then layer by layer rebuilt the heifer's opened flank. We were doing great. I was proud of my brave little heifer, proud of my two untrained assistants and really prouder of me than I was of them or the cow!

Now keep in mind, we were in a big old cattle barn. There was no electricity or lights overhead. In the loft above us, a flock of chickens were scratching and pecking in the hay for seeds. The dust they stirred up was filtering down through the cracks to the dirt floor—my barnyard operating room!

I finally managed to get the wound all together and threaded my big, curved suture needle with some cotton suture tape. I tried to push the needle through the skin but the hide was too tough. Try after try, my needle and needle holder just couldn't take the strain. I was at a loss and was sure I was about to lose my good surgical image. Making small talk, and trying to come up with a reasonable answer, I jokingly said how nice it would be to have a leather punch.

Tony Arnett came to my rescue. "Just a minute, Doc, we got one here in the harness room." He went into the room got the punch and at my direction dropped it into the can of water and disinfectant.

After I thought it was reasonably sterile, I fished it out and punched holes up each edge of the skin incision and laced up that big wound with my suture tape just like you would a pair of shoes! I then salved over the wound with an antibiotic cream, gave the cow some penicillin and dispensed a sulfa drug for Tony to give her twice a day. By this time the cow, with all of that pressure relieved in her belly, was bright eyed and, in spite of her still paralyzed condition from the spinal anesthetic, was trying to lick her newborn calf!

I cleaned up my mess, loaded the gear into my car and completed my visit. Inwardly I was really elated. The world, or at least the world of cow caesareans at that time, was my oyster!

After Reverend Owney and I discussed the care of the cow and her calf, he walked with me toward my car. When we were almost there he stopped and, turning to me, very quietly asked, "Doctor Martin, did you ever do one of these operations before?"

Just as quietly I said, "No,"

We both laughed out loud. Believe it or not, two days later I did my second c-section on a cow just two miles from the Owney farm. It went just as well, chickens, dirty barn, dust and all!

§   §   §

Charles Montague and his brother Roland originate from old-time set-tlers here in northern Kentucky. They sold (and still sell) insurance and real estate which, during this time, included what was left of the Montague acre-age now surrounded by the city limits of our town. To begin the develop-ment of this tract of land, they built a street through the middle of this property and named it after President Jackson. On one side of Jackson Street Roland has a nice little barn and at that time raised Hampshire hogs, black pigs with a white band around their neck. On the other side of the street brother Charles operated a small dairy and milked Holstein cows, the big black ones with white markings or white with black—whatever! I did a lot of work for both brothers, who have become life long friends. Charles, in particular, thought I had the most exciting and fascinating job in the world and insisted I call him any time I wanted company on my farm visits. I took advantage of his friendship and his volunteering instincts on many occa-sions. Charles often referred to our excursions to the farms as little adven-tures. Now, looking back on these episodes, I have to agree.

Charles Monatague's humor, hobbies, general knowledge and hill coun-try heritage are unmatched. He and I are about the same age, but he is about an inch or two taller than I am. He is a sporty dresser, always wearing a business suit accentuated with a fancy button-up vest that contains in its pocket a large pocket watch dressed up with a fancy fob. Charles speaks with a slight nasal drawl, his thin lips pulling out one word at a time. His dry sense of humor is an adjunct to his constant string of hill-country stories. Besides his interest in his dairy and cows, he is an avid steamboat enthusiast and is in his glory here on the banks of the busy Ohio River, recognizing every boat as it announces itself by its steam whistle.

I had a late afternoon phone call, with the usual, "Hurry up, Doc," again to attend a heifer unable to deliver her calf. The owner, John, lived on Big Cat Creek in Lawrence County at the very beginning of the big hills. John was not the best farmer around, deploring the hard manual labor that made a farm a success. Instead, he was content to trade a few hogs and cows with his neighbors and at the local stock yard. He also was adept at directing his wife's efforts as she did the gardening and fed the livestock. John's main attribute was that he was the best cusser in all of northern Kentucky, unable to say one sentence without uttering an oath. Besides the "Hurry up, Doc," part of his conversation he included, ". . . the damned heifer can't have her damned calf. Hell, Doc, come on up here." I got the picture.

I called Charles Montague and asked him if he wanted to go with me. In less than a heartbeat, he said, "I sure do, what have we got this time?" In a few minutes I picked him up and we started on our way to Cussin' John's, a name even his neighbors tagged him with.

I drove as fast as I could, hoping to get there before dark, since the rural electric system hadn't found Big Cat Creek yet and my flashlight was a poor substitute for light. For that matter, John had to drive ten miles to Louisa, the county seat, to use a phone to call me. It was a very isolated part of the county.

Here in what some call Appalachia, these isolated areas still flourish. The habits and ways of the residents' lives are pretty similar, with some more successful than others in their endeavors. They marry within their area, and I learned in the very beginning of my time here in this land to never talk about somebody because nearly everybody around here is "kin."

Charles and I pulled up in front of John's barn. It was across the road from the old two-story farm house. John and his wife were sitting on the porch waiting and waved as we stopped the car and got out. Charles, making himself useful, got the obstetrical kit out of the car. He knew the routine. My kit included four "OB" chains with handles, a stainless steel bucket and the usual soap, disinfectants, towels and rubber obstetrical sleeves. It also included a small block and tackle I used to help extract my babies. and a large bottle of mineral oil, messy as it was, for a lubricant.

By this time John had arrived at our car and we were greeted with, "Hi, Doc, I'm damn sure glad you're here. We've had a hell of a time with that damned little old cow. Fact is, Mack's been workin' on her fer over a hour. He says she's too damned little to have this damned calf."

At the mention of Mack, I glanced at my friend. We knew Mack was the local "cow doctor." I called them "quacks" and tolerated them because once in a while, when they failed—and they usually did—they called me in on their "case." And then again, if you said anything bad about them, chances are your were talking to "kin."

Charles turned to John and asked, "Where is the cow?"

"The son-of-a-bitch is back there in the damned barn, clean back in the last stall."

"John, get me some hot water and some clean towels. Better bring a bar of Ivory soap if you have it." John took my bucket and crossed the road to get my water. Montague and I picked up the equipment and with the aid of my big flashlight, headed into the depths of the big, dark barn. While we were looking for our patient, Charles again asked me about the charlatan, Mack. I told him Mack was a friend of John's and everybody else on the creek. I also explained that he generally saw these cases before I did, had no conception of sanitation or cleanliness and, invariably, added more problems to my work. I didn't spend too much time ruminating about Mack. I had dealt with him before and knew it was better to ignore him and try to undo his mistakes.

By this time Charles and I had walked to the back of the barn to look for our laboring patient. I flashed the light around and there huddled up in the corner was a tiny little cow, not much bigger than a good-sized calf. I continued to search other stalls when my friend spoke up with his particular nasal tone of voice and said, "Doc, I think that little cow is the one that's trying to have the calf!" Sure enough, he was right, bathed in the beam of my flashlight was the smallest pregnant heifer I had ever seen. It was like a calf trying to have a calf. She was a little Jersey, so young her horns had only grown an inch or two from her head. We both whistled in disbelief and I knew it would take some kind of skill, or magic, maybe both, to solve this problem.

"Montague, you grab her legs and let's see if we can get her out of here in some light so we can see." There was just an iota of daylight left. We both grabbed a leg and pulled her down the hallway out into the fading twilight. I noticed as we dragged her along, a tiny foot protruded from her birth canal. I also noticed the mother's big soulful eyes. It was as if she was pleading with us to help her.

John hadn't come back with the water and while we waited, Charles asked what I thought we should do. I suggested since she was so tiny, we both might be able to lift her bodily by her rear legs, at least high enough I could pour a pint of mineral oil into her for lubrication. He grabbed her back legs, and with a strain lifted her up enough and I poured in the oil. I put the empty bottle down and got one of her legs and together he and I lifted her a little higher. The oil flowed by gravity into the womb. As we did this, the calf fell toward the cow's head into the uterus and the tiny leg and hoof disappeared.

I quickly put on my long sleeved obstetrical glove, cleaned up the expectant mother and examined her. Blessings, now I could feel both of the unborn's front legs and its head. I realized we solved Mack's delivery problem when the calf was swallowed back into its mother's womb and the head straightened to a normal delivery position.

"Charles, if you can, hold her up and I will get these chains on the baby's legs and head and maybe," I paused while I strained to get my chains on, "we can deliver this calf." The heifer about this time gave a loud bawl, forced a mighty uterine contraction and the head and legs presented themselves! Charles let go of the cow's legs and helped me pull on the chains and in less time that it takes to tell about it, we had a tiny, still alive, baby bull calf on the ground. The mother's big dark eyes again got my attention as if she were trying to thank us for helping her. I got that strange, wonderful feeling that came over me when I brought new life into the world.

I looked up toward the house and there came John running as fast as he could across the road, steaming water splashing from a bucket in each hand. Under his arms were some clean rags. Floating in one of the buckets was big bar of Ivory soap. Everything I ordered had arrived. "Doc Martin, here's that damned hot water and stuff you ordered me to git fer ya." With that remark he stopped and stared at the little cow and her tiny calf and realized my magic had worked. For once, John was speechless. I attended the cow and calf and left instructions with John's wife on the aftercare, because I knew if it was to be done, she would be the one to do it. Charles by now had the instruments washed and back in my car. John reached down in the bib of his overalls, got out his checkbook and I filled out the check with a stub of a pencil he offered. He managed to sign the check, I thanked him and got in the car. My last comment was a suggestion he not call Mack for his help anymore.

We left Cussin' John's place and drove out the gravel road to the mouth of Big Cat Creek at the main highway. Charles asked me, "Doc, why do you put up with those 'old pappy men'?" Now I had heard that expression used before and knew it was what a lot of the hill folks called the untrained, homemade veterinarians that I referred to as quacks. I don't know where the term came from but you can bet it was a real part of the Appalachian dictionary.

"You know, Charles, I don't mind them around. Certainly they don't hurt me and of course, in the long run, their lack of knowledge helps me. But it does concern me deeply because their ways are costly to my clients and God knows these poor people don't need that kind of liability." After a pause I went on, "But on the other hand until we trained professionals came along, that's all the farmer had."

"Just how many of these quacks, as you call them, or old pappy men are around here?"

"There is one in nearly every neighborhood and the farther you get back into the hill country, the more of them are around. Some of the farmers even say some are, '. . . real good vet'narys.' Now I have told you about Mack, let me tell you about one closer to home. His name is Roy Lester. But first, let's stop at this little filling-station-grocery-store down the road and get some gasoline. It would be a long dark walk if we ran out!" Charles agreed. I stopped at the store, bought some gasoline and got us each a candy bar to tide us over 'till we got back to town. Of course I had a little social visit with the proprietor, as was expected, before we were again started on our way home.

"What about this Roy Lester you were getting ready to tell me about?" As we drove away from the country store, I started my story.

"When I first came to Ashland, I heard stories about Roy every day—mostly after I was called to straighten out his mistakes. I never did meet him face to face. He always managed to disappear before I got there."

One farmer friend, Doug George, told me when I inquired, "Mr. Lester," that's what he insisted people call him, ". . . just left when I told him I called you. He said he was needed some t'other place, quick."

Another one of my good clients, one of the Cooksey boys, commented when I opened my medical bag to get some medicine for his sick mule, "Mr. Lester's got a black bag too, Doc. Its a helluva lot bigger than the one you 're a-totin'. Funny thing though, he never lets nobody see what's in it."

I continued my story. "I went on my rounds for months, never letting Roy Lester or any other of the neighborhood quacks bother me. Matter of fact, I found it to my advantage to praise them at times, knowing they would soon get the word and stop belittling me to my clients. One cold, rainy morning I was called to Cooksey's place to treat a cow with milk fever. When I got there I found the cow on her feet but very unsteady. She was standing straddle-legged, obviously in a lot of discomfort. Her udder looked like it was about to burst. There was a rag tied around each teat, so tight the ends of the teats were purple from lack of blood circulation. I knew then Roy Lester had been there and maybe, in spite of his lack of education, probably saved this cow's life by pumping her udder full of air with a tire pump and then tying the teats closed to keep the air from escaping." I went on to explain to Charles that this trick simply held the milk in the udder, and the cow reabsorbed her own nutrients from the calcium in her system. It was an old time treatment and I saw a lot of this in the first days of my practice. As I busied myself untying the rags, I asked Cooksey to get the big brown bottle of medicine out of my medical bag. I got the rags untied and was busy massaging the cow's udder and, while I was doing that, I asked him to also get me the bottle of skin disinfectant and the rubber hose outfit I used to inject the medicine in the cow's jugular vein. He handed them both to me. Cooksey said to me, "Doc, you sure carry a lot of stuff in that black bag. You know, t'other day Mr. Lester was here and when he took off around the barn to pee, I snuck a look in his doctor's bag just to see what was there. You know what I found?" And before I could answer, he said, "that big old bag he totes around had nothin' in it except a bunch of old wadded up newspapers."

Most of my farm clients eventually heard about Roy's black bag and most made a point, just like they had never been fooled by him, to tell me they knew all along he didn't have anything in it. My coming to Ashland was the beginning of his demise and by the time I stopped doing large animal practice, not very many people remembered old Roy. Roy Lester passed away some years later and, believe it or not, I missed him. He was always a source of entertainment and conversation for me.

We were almost back to town when I finished telling my friend this story and all of this time he never uttered a word. He was absolutely fascinated by the ways of some of the hill country people, the quacks, or as he called them the old pappy men. It was hard for him to believe there were people like Roy Lester this close to our modern town.

As a matter of interest, about two weeks after Charles and I delivered the calf at Cussin' John's, I was called to one of John's neighbors to see a sick mule. Again I called Charles Montague and again he jumped at the chance to go on the call. When we got there Mack was there too, doctoring my patient! When I finished the job, he mentioned the small heifer and the fancy obstetrical work I did. He told me he had just come back from John's just a few minutes earlier where he delivered a calf from another laboring cow! In the same breath, he thanked me for the use of my mineral oil trick with the remark, ". . . I use it all the time now."

My good friend just stood there and stared in amazement and when we were on our way home he said, "Doc, what goes on in this country with all of these superstitions, country tricks and characters?"

With not a bit of hesitation, I gave him my answer. I asked if he remembered the story about Granny Rice and the c-section my daughter Terri and I did on Granny's sow.

"Sure do," he said, "but what's this got to do with what we were talking about?"

And then I reminded him what Granny Rice told me that pretty spring day up on her mountain. She said, "Doctor Martin, you know this all has to be part of God's Plan."

So that's the only reason I could think of.

THE NEW LOOK

CLIENT EDUCATION SEEMED TO BE WORKING. MORE AND MORE FARMERS came to me for advice about their animals. Advice was free and I never refused to talk to anyone who came seeking my opinions or suggestions for an animal's care. Their ideas and attitudes were changing along with the times, though I was sure there were still witches out there, and I knew for a fact there were still "old pappy men." Neither concerned me anymore and I wasn't very surprised when I heard of some strange happenings on the farms.

My practice was doing well, covering a tremendous area that included farms in southern Ohio, western West Virginia and, of course, Kentucky. At the same time I came to Kentucky, Dr. Louis Motycka, a classmate of mine in college, started a mixed animal practice in Ironton, Ohio. Dr. Owen Karr (thirty-five miles west in my old hometown, Portsmouth) also treated large animals. There were two other veterinarians in Ashland. Dr. George Borst, an excellent veterinarian, limited himself to small animal medicine only. The other man, Dr. Wallace, an older doctor with older ways and a very small practice did some farm work and treated an occasional cat or dog. We waved as we passed in our cars, but only once did I ever talk to him face to face. He died shortly after we came to Ashland. No one replaced him.

To the south, all the way to the Tennessee state line, there were no college-graduated, licensed veterinarians! To the west, excepting Karr in southern Ohio, there was not another veterinarian between Ashland and Mount Sterling, Kentucky, a small town seventy five miles from me. This tremendous expanse of territory and the demand for up-to-date animal management and care came to be more than I could handle. The unimproved roads took their toll on my automobiles. A car wouldn't last more than a year and then it had to be replaced. The unbelievable long hours and hard physical work had me believing I wouldn't last much longer either, unless some drastic changes were made.

Veterinary medicine was coming into a new era. The type of work I was doing the hills had to be changed. Besides the huge area, which was defeating me, there was the matter of economics. Inflated dollars necessitated that I charge more for my services. Case in point, my first auto cost twelve hundred dollars—the new ones, in the 1950s, were over two thousand! Inflation never approached the farmer's cow; she was still marketed at pre-war figures. If I was to survive, I would have to compete with the changing economics, helping me and, at the same time, helping my clients.

While I was still in the university, most of us had thoughts about future homes and of course office facilities. I, too, made those plans, particularly about my office. I had visions of a combination small animal and large animal facility. The advantages were obvious. If I could entice the farmer to bring his ailing animal to me, I could charge him reasonable fees for state-of-the -art veterinary medicine, avoid the travel expense and time involved covering the huge area. I had no intention of telling my clients I would make more money! What I did tell them was I could do my work for a lot less money. I found a tract of land consisting of ten surveyed lots on a dirt road with no city sewers or city water service. This was in a new sub-division just recently annexed by the city. It had one more plus for me, the property was just across the road from Pidge Mohr's horse barn!

I talked to the city manager who assured me if I would build my clinic, the city would supply the sewer and water service. This was the beginning of the Martin Veterinary Clinic, which I built in 1952. It consisted of a main office building with kennels for cats and dogs, a combination large and small animal surgery and a five-stall barn to house my sick large animal patients. The lots involved in this complex were divided into paddocks and enclosed with board fences. It was a fancy place, dripping with the atmosphere of beautiful fancy-fenced horse farms in the Blue Grass section of the state. My new clinic was one of the first large and small animal clinics ever built in Kentucky. Several veterinarians visited me, saw the advantages and later built similar facilities.

Now I had the new look, and the clinic was a great success. I added to the new look by pursuing the small animal business, since I now had an excellent place to house the cats and dogs.

The post-war years saw many changes. Farm kids that went away to war came back wiser and older—seeing the need for something better than scratching a living out of the dirt. Veterans took advantage of government-sponsored education, and many farm boys went to the universities and studied. Some became engineers, some teachers, while others earned degrees in agriculture. These people came back to the farms with their new knowledge and new ideas. While our people were getting smarter, the physical state of our area was dramatically improved. Some of the graveled roads were getting a coat of asphalt and the telephone company and the rural electric companies were expanding their services to the remote areas. What a blessing—the hill country was getting a face lift! The stereotype of Appalachia would have to disappear.

In spite of all this grandeur, at the new clinic not every case could be transported to me, and I still spent many hours on the road, working as hard as ever, and experiencing more exciting, and often frustrating, occurrences.

§   §   §

Mrs. Bob McGlothlin phoned very early one spring morning and told me they had a cow in labor and needed my services. I added their name to the growing list of things to do and places in which to do them. Bob, a post-war University of Kentucky agricultural school graduate, and his wife operated a modern dairy farm, one of the better ones in the county. He was following in his father's footsteps by operating the farm.

Generally I organized my visits so I didn't have to backtrack, but emergencies always came first. My list for the day already included a cow paralyzed with milk fever at the Ernest Bonzo dairy in Greenup County. Mrs. George Davis had a cow to have her afterbirth removed and Walter Stewart called and said he had some calves, "with the murn." This was a hill country term for bloody diarrhea or, using another bit of local color, the "scours." Bonzo's place was in the opposite direction from the other two places, and since his case was the most urgent, this would be my first stop. I also thought it would be wise to give Bob's cow some more time. Maybe she would have her calf by herself before I got there. This latter proved to be wishful think-ing!

A quick check of my car for an ample supply of medicines and supplies prompted me to go back into the office to pick up some more milk fever medicine and some antibiotics for Walter Stewart's calves. Just before leav-ing I told my office manager, Stormy Lemaster (he told me he was named Stormy because he was born on a stormy night) where I would be during the day. He could call me at any of the places on the list, and I would call him when I was finished with the last call.

Ernest Bonzo's cow was in the barn, stretched out unconscious on the floor, a classical case of "post parturient paresis," or as we all called it, milk fever. She was a big Holstein cow, a heavy milker and a real money maker. These heavy milkers were always the ones that suffered from this discom-fort.

Ernest Bonzo was a very good farmer, short in stature, demanding in voice and very proud of what he and his family had done. He had few friends, was at odds with some of his family, and gave many the impression he dis-trusted them. He was guarded when he talked to you, often to the point of being gruff, but he never let you forget what a good operation he had or how hard he and his family worked to get it. All of them, including boss Ernest himself, were up before dawn and still hard at it when dark came. He loved the farm he owned and rented. It was a very big operation. However his real love was money. The farms made it for him and he was very frugal when it came to the dollar. When I got there to see this cow I am sure his worry was for the cash, not so much for his cow. He never intimidated me. I approached him like he approached me—honest and straightforward. In spite of his differences with others, he and his entire family became my friends and I enjoyed many professional visits to their farm. This friendship exists to this day.

I examined my patient, assured myself of the diagnosis and went to work, putting the nose lead in her nose. This piece of equipment was like the ring farmers put in a bull's nose only shaped in this case like a pair of pliers with a rope through the handles. With it, I could control the cow's head move-ments when I worked on her. I instructed Bonzo to stand on the rope to hold her head down, even though she was unconscious at the time.

As I have said, the milk fever treatment usually has magic-like, dramatic results. The cow often gets on her feet, or can try to get up, before the treatment is finished. Satisfied that Mr. Bonzo could hold her, I applied an antiseptic over part of the neck, knelt down, put the needle into the jugular vein and started my medicine on its way. I stood up, looped the long rubber tubing around the cow's ear to keep it steady, and with my knee pressed against her chest, I monitored her heart beat. She began shaking, a good sign she was responding to the medicine. It wasn't long before she opened her eyes.

I am sure by now Bonzo was convinced his cow was going to live and the urgency of the case was gone. He let his mind wander to other things. On this farm they kept several Holstein bulls for breeders. They were high-priced, well-bred animals, all capable of improving the qualities of their offspring. He started to tell me about the one in the lot next to where I was working. Completely forgetting what we were doing, he stepped off the rope and started over to look and brag on the bull. By now the cow, still in a stupor, was struggling and flailing her legs, bawling and trying to find her newborn calf. Before I could stop Bonzo, the cow tossed her head and I was hit in the face with the heavy nose lead! I yelled at Ernest, said a few really good cuss words, dropped the bottle of medicine and clapped my hands to my eye and my face. I was really hurt. Ernest came running, at the same time apologizing and yelling, "Doc, can I do anything?"

Almost in a state of shock, I exploded and said, "Hell no, just stand on the damned rope and help me treat the cow." Finally I had nerve enough to take my hands away from my face expecting the worse and found the moisture was tears, not blood. To make it short, I ended up with a really good black eye, a well cow and a stern bit of advice from Ernest Bonzo to be more careful in the future! I went to his milk house and washed my face in cold water, checked it for damage and called Stormy at the office. Nothing else had come in. All this time Ernest was standing there looking at me with a somber stare. I am not sure what he was thinking and then he asked me how much he owed me. I told him and, after a moments hesitation, he dug into his wallet and handed me a crumpled ten dollar bill.

My next stop was at Walter Stewart's place to treat his sick calves. By this time my head ached and my face was starting to swell. Walter offered his sympathy and suggested I go home and come back at a later time, but I thanked him for his thoughts, telling him I still had a lot of work ahead of me. Walter purchased these calves from the stockyard, and like most stock-yard critters, they were exposed to many infectious diseases even though the sale barns were kept reasonably clean and a veterinarian was in attendance at all times. One of the diseases frequently contracted by the young animals was a bacterial infection that caused a bloody diarrhea. This is what Walter diagnosed over the phone as the bloody murn. I examined the calves and discussed the problem with him, and while I was talking about them, I gave each an injection of an antibiotic. I dispensed some medicine to give the calves later and suggested he buy his calves directly from a farmer instead of through the market. The calves responded to treatment, all recovered, and Walter Stewart became a good client as well as a friend. This was just a routine call to me but to the Stewarts, it was a relief to know their calves were all right. Just as I was getting into my car to go on to attend Mrs. Davis's cow, Walter's wife came to the car and told me my office had called. Mrs. McGlothlin was wondering why I was taking so long to get to their farm. Stormy assured them I was on my way.

§   §   §

Mrs. Davis was patiently waiting when I drove into her driveway. I knew she would have the cow in the barn ready for me. Her husband, like many others in the community, worked in town at the steel mill and did his farming after work. She saw me drive in and met me at the barn with a bucket of warm water, some towels and soap. I appreciated that gesture but she mentioned something about, "Ladies and . . . this sort of thing . . . just wasn't proper." I agreed. She went back to the house, I cleaned the cow. I looked around the barn and finally found a pitch fork and carried the now-expelled placenta around to the back of the barn. Mr. Davis could dispose of it when he got home from work. With seven dollars in my pocket—a good fee in those days—I hurried to my car and drove on to my next call, the cow trying to have her calf.

§   §   §

The McGlothlin dairy was a first-class operation. Bob had the cow in a clean calving stall. Plenty of hot water was available in the milk house and a new bar of soap and a stack of clean towels were at my disposal. We tied the cow's halter rope to a post in the barn and after washing her birthing end, I examined her and at once realized this would be no ordinary delivery. As soon as I put my gloved arm into her she would strain, bawl and try to lie down. After a while of feeling for the calf and her straining and getting up and down, dragging me with her, I finally determined the calf was backwards with both feet tucked up under its belly. This was a true breech presentation. I tried my very hardest to push the calf forward so I could grasp one of its legs and straighten it out. Every time I pushed, she would bawl, give a mighty contraction and fall to the floor. Once more, down again I would go with no progress made at all.

Nearly an hour went by and now my eye was almost swollen closed, and my headache was worse than ever. I was bruised all over and my arm was sore and raw from my ups and downs with this animal. I had to stop and rest. After a few minutes I tried again.

The next hour was a repeat of the first. If the cow would just cooperate it appeared I had a routine breech delivery but at this point I had gained nothing. Finally with a mighty loud bawl and a tremendous contraction, she expelled the contents of her bowels all over me, fell to the ground and stayed there! At this point I had gained nothing. Nearly exhausted, I was covered with fresh cow manure, birthing fluids and dirt from head to toe. My arm and fingers were numb and my headache told me to stop. I did. Bob and I agreed we needed a different approach. He also agreed with me when I remarked, "This is sure one damned hard way to make a living."

As exasperated as he was over my hopefully temporary failure, he said, "Doc, take a break. I'll be back in a minute and we will try again." His suggestion to take a break was like music from the angels. It was heavenly! I went into the milk house and tried to clean myself up as best I could while he was gone. By chance I happened to look at a pile of old farm implements and noticed a singletree from a horse-drawn wagon. Suddenly a new plan came to me.

Before I could say anything, Bob came back from the house with two glasses, a pitcher of cold well water and a pint of Old Yellowstone Bourbon Whiskey. I was already thinking his suggestion was better than the one I had in mind about delivering the calf. Now I always made it a point never to drink with a client unless it was in my house. This time I made the exception. While we were sipping the "Yallerstone," I told him about the singletree and my plan. Grasping at any straw, we both agreed it was worth a try. We poured ourselves another drink from the pint bottle, and in a few minutes I went to my car and got the big heavy cotton rope I used for a casting harness for horses. I tied the rope around the cow's rear feet and then, with the same rope, fastened each end of the singletree to her ankles. This spread the cow's legs wide apart. Together we managed to loop a chain over a rafter above us and hooked my block and tackle to this and the middle of the leg spreader.

We pulled the ropes and hoisted her rear end off of the ground. The cow, now as exhausted as we were, was quiet and stopped her straining. As we elevated her body the calf moved forward in the uterus and gave me some room to work. I poured a pint of my lubricating mineral oil into her, found first one hind foot and straightened it out, then I did the other one the same way. Quickly I fastened the obstetrical chains to both hind legs and fastened them to the same rafter with the block and tackle with a third chain. Then Bob and I gently lowered the cow to the floor. As she went down, the calf, which was dead, slipped from the womb. We untied the cow and with a lot of tender loving care on the part of the McGlothlins, she made an uneventful recovery. Once again ingenuity made its play and the day was saved. The singletree became standard equipment in my obstetrical kit and was used in many calving cases over the years.

I put my dirty equipment in my bucket and went into the milk house and washed myself all over with the hose. My filthy coveralls and dirty undershirt went in the bucket with the instruments. It had been one hell of a hard day. I was completely exhausted, filthy dirty, my head seemed like it was going to split and it was all I could do to see out of my swollen black eye. My arms and my hands were nearly numb from manipulating the calf.

As I started out the door, Bob said, "Doctor, I sure want to praise you for your hard work and thinking about that wagon part." Even in my poor physical shape of the moment I appreciated his kind word. And then he said, "There is still enough water in this pitcher to wash down one more shot of Old Yellowstone." His suggestion once again sounded pretty reasonable. We finished off the water, and the Old Yellowstone too.

There was a telephone in the milk house and I called Stormy back in my office. He had no more for me to do and asked my what kind of a day I had. I said, "Not too much to get excited about, I'll give you the details when I get to the office." I got in my car and drove back to town.

A Changing Time

In a few days I recovered from the discomforts earned at Bonzo's farm and the McGlothlin dairy. They were just temporary physical inconveniences.

On a warm Saturday morning, after a hard work week, I looked forward to the week's end and some rest. It never happened that way—I had an accident.

Officer Miles, the dispatcher at the police barracks called me and said Chris Crank at Cannonsburg had a very sick cow. He also told me that Mr. Crank wanted me, ". . . to come right away." Miles laughed; he had heard that many times before. Crank's small farm was only five miles from the police barracks on a little side road, close to my friend Henri Riekert's place. I knew exactly where to go.

I stopped my car in front of an old weather-beaten wooden barn across the road from Mr. Crank's house. I blew my car horn to announce my arrival and in an instant the house door opened. An old man waved his cane in my direction and with a weak, gravely voice said, "I'll be with ya, soon as I get my coat."

In just a short time here came my client, slowly hobbling across the road, walking laboriously with the aid of a cane in each hand. He was so crippled, every step he took appeared to be his last! When he finally got to the barnyard, leaning on one cane to steady himself and pointing toward the back of the barn with the other, he said to me in a low, almost inaudible voice, "She's back in the back of the barn with her new calf." Sure enough over in one corner of the old barn was a little Jersey cow, collapsed with her head twisted under her body. Her legs were sticking out into the air like broomsticks. She was bloated big, like a full tick on a hound dog! By her side was a tiny baby calf, its big brown eyes blinking at me, no doubt wondering what this new world was all about. It was obvious Mr. Crank's cow was a milk fever victim, seriously complicated with the bloat.

It was my habit to never take any equipment or medicine to the animal until I looked at it, then I would go to my car and get what I needed. This gave me time to do my thinking and get my game plan organized for the case. I learned this trick when I worked for Dr. Karr in Portsmouth back in my intern days. This day was no different. I went to the car for the medicine. On the way out of the barn Chris Crank sighed and apologized, "Doctor, I'm sorry, I ain't much help to ya." That was obvious. Without his walking canes he was, to all appearances, immobile!

Before I could treat this animal, I had to get her head out from under her body. Crank was no help, he could hardly walk, much less lift. I was young and strong, and without any hesitation I grabbed the cow by her horns and gave a mighty heave. The head came free but the instant I lifted her, my back cracked with an audible sound and I fell to the floor! I experienced excruciating pain! Mr. Crank was beside himself. He dropped both of his canes and ran four or five steps into the stall to help me. His whisper was gone. In a near booming voice he shouted, "Oh my goodness, Doctor, let me help ya!" Waving him away and wincing with the severe pain, by now almost unbearable, I managed to tell him I thought I was alright. He leaned over and helped me get back on my feet. Somehow I managed to treat the animal and as my milk fever medicine did its magic, she started to recover. With a loud rumble she belched and after a huge rush of gas deflated her, she was back to her normal size.

I wondered how bad I was hurt. In my mind I imagined a torn ligament or at the worst, a broken vertebra. Mr. Crank helped me to my car, managing his mobility very well. Once he was satisfied I could drive myself home, he picked up his walking canes and slowly hobbled back across the road to his house!

I suffered the agonies of hell for a few days, though I went to my doctor friend, Harry Stone, and he prescribed some medicine and insisted I get some bed rest to relax the muscles. He thought I had possibly ruptured a vertebral disc or probably sustained a slight fracture. Years later doctors at the Mayo Clinic substantiated Harry Stone's diagnosis. In a week or so I was back to near normal but Chris Crank's cow had done me in. I suffered with this ailment for many years, and it was one of the reasons I eventually retired.

§   §   §

Willa Fay Vanhoose, Lofty's wife, called me and said they needed me. "Doc, have a cow about to be fresh, can you come help?" The Vanhoose dairy was on Big Garner Creek Road. This was one of my very best farming communities, and I worked for everyone in the area. It was as if we were almost a great big family.

When Charles Montague, my insurance-selling friend, heard I was hurt at Mr. Crank's, he called to offer condolences and to volunteer his help if I ever needed him. I was slowly recovering from my back injury when Willa Fay called about their cow. I decided this would be a good time to take advantage of Montague's offer. I phoned him at his office and he jumped at the chance to go with me. Friends like him were worth their weight in gold!

It was a rain-swept, gusty April day, with thunder rumbling in the distance as storms drifted across the hills. The creeks were almost out of their banks but the weather had warmed some and the trees were starting to get their leaves back. Other than the hard rain, it was a good time to be out. Every thing seemed OK but three days earlier driving on a seldom used overgrown narrow road to a farmer's barn, a low hanging branch caught one of the windshield wiper blades and broke it off. I kept saying to myself, ". . . get it fixed," but I never got around to it. The broken wiper didn't make it any easier seeing as it scratched back and forth across the glass windshield.

As you can imagine, farm practice was hard, and most places I worked were not what you might call the finest of farm operations. My friends and neighbors in my area did not live the life of the aristocratic farmer in the Blue Grass section of the state. The barns here were often converted pole buildings, mainly used for hanging and curing tobacco. Some were old log barns left over from their father's and grandfather's days, some rotting and about to fall down—almost a hazard to work in. Mud, filth and dust was the rule. Until just recently sanitation was almost unheard of.

Lofty's dairy was different. It was one of the shining stars of the dairy community, with the dairy barn clean and modern. The Vanhooses always had plenty of good help, and it was a pleasure to work there.

Charles and I drove up the hill and nearly into the barn so we would not get soaked by the cloudburst rain hitting on the metal barn roof like hail. I grabbed my medical bag off the back seat of my car and both of us, trying to dodge the huge raindrops, ran into the barn. I said my hellos and introduced my friend to Mant, Lofty's brother, and to Willa Fay, queen of the household. Lofty was in the milk house getting hot water and clean towels so they would be ready for me. Every electric light in the barn was turned on. The clean concrete floor was covered with a fine coating of white lime that was supposed to be a sterilizing agent. There was some question about its efficiency but take your choice. You either smelled the sharp odor of the lime or the pungent odor of the cow manure. Two buckets of steaming hot water, a big bar of soap and a bundle of towels were in the aisle waiting for me.

The cow was ready too. She was a great big Holstein in prime condition but obviously very heavy with her unborn calf. Mant had her in the barn with her head fastened in one of the stanchions. The mud and manure had been scraped from her hips and her tail and she had been washed with soap and water. She seemed content—until she had a labor contraction. Then she stomped her feet and bellowing loudly, strained hard and tried to expel her calf. When the labor pain quit, she relaxed and chewed her cud like a normal cow!

I slipped on my boots and coveralls and tied the cow's tail around to her side with a piece of string from a bale of hay. I scrubbed her some more with some surgical soap and was ready for my examination. Just then the lightning flashed and the boom of the thunder shook the barn. Momentarily, the lights went out, the rain was crashing on the barn roof and for an instant, everything stopped. Willa Fay gasped, Lofty said, "Well I'll be damned!" In a matter of seconds the lights were back on, nothing was wrong and, in spite of the confusion, the cow stood contently and chewed her cud! Willa Fay was calm now and Lofty made no comment except to say, "That lightning hit close by." I put on my obstetrical glove, really just a rubber glove with a long sleeve that came clear to my shoulder, and inserted my hand and arm into the cow's vagina. It was no wonder she couldn't deliver. The calf was a breech with its legs tucked up under its body.

The Vanhoose boys, like most of the farmers, were pretty good at deliveries but they didn't know how to handle this one. Mant made the remark, "Doc, it ain't got no head." I silently agreed with him, at least it had no head on that end of its body.

I began my work with a flowery dissertation on proper calving, good dairy farm management, the nasty April storms and anything else I could think about. I always talked a lot to the client when I was working on his or her animal. It kept them quiet and gave me more time to figure things out without giving the impression I was fumbling. My tactic usually worked very well.

In the meantime, Charles had put the OB chains and handles into one of the buckets of hot water and added some disinfectant to it.

The cow was an older animal with no history of previous birthing problems. This breech calf was just something that happened once in a while. Confiding with myself, I figured this would be an easy case and a chance to enhance my already good image. I rattled on with my conversation, everyone listening to what I had to say about the cow. I acted like I was having a hard time while I pushed the baby forward and repositioned one of its legs. Then with another push forward, I got the other leg straightened out and put one of my obstetrical chains around each foot. Now instead of being up under its body, the calf's legs were stretched out behind it, ready for a normal delivery. I told Mant and Lofty to pull on the chains and with just a little effort, and a big contraction from the cow, the calf was born, and lay on the floor blinking its eyes. Mant pulled it out of the way and was busy with a feed sack wiping it off and rubbing it dry. The mother seemed to be relieved. The rain was coming down even harder than ever, and between thunderclaps, the lights would go out for an instant and then come back on. All this time my friend Charles never said a single word.

After I delivered a newborn animal, I always examined the mother and medicated her to prevent any complications. Just as I inserted my arm back into the cow with a fist full of antibiotic tablets, Charles, always one to make a joke, said, "Doc, don't go gettin' greedy, what are you goin' to do, try and get another one?" I didn't have time to respond to his joke because, sure enough, when I went back in her, there was another calf! Once again I did the chain maneuvering and in short order had the calf on the floor with its twin. This time when I examined the cow she was empty.

I was through. It had been an easy delivery for me, a surprising one for the Vanhooses and a good show for my insurance-selling friend. Mant had all of the equipment washed and dried and in my medical bag. I took off my coveralls, washed myself in the milk house, disinfected my boots and tossed the dirty coveralls in the bag with my instruments.

Willa Fay had the check book in her hand and before paying me thanked me for coming and offered us a cup of hot coffee. I thanked her but told her we wanted to go on home since it was late—almost dark. I did ask her if I could use the phone and she said, "Try the one in the milk house."

I called my office and Stormy told us he had one more stop for us to make. The caller had a cow he thought was snake bitten and needed us. Stormy, mimicking the caller's voice, said, "Right away, her udders swolled like it's goin' to bust." I got the directions and told Stormy to go on home as it was getting late. "Doc, one more thing before you hang up," I waited for the 'one more thing.' "The man sounded to me like he was real drunk, slurring his words and demanded you get to him with the snake bite medicine as soon as you could. I told him it would be after dark before you could get there. He said that'd be all right but he needed you no matter what time." I thanked Stormy and ran through the rain to my car where Charles was already waiting. We waved, turned the car around and drove down the county road toward the main highway.

Charles tamped some tobacco into his pipe, lighted it with a big country match and after a few puffs to be sure it was all fired up, he turned, and looking me straight in the face he asked, "Doc, did you know there was another calf in that cow?"

I knew that question had to come up sooner or later and laughing out loud I answered him, "Charles, I was just as surprised as you were. I found it when I went back to put the antibiotics in her uterus!"

It had been an easy job. I was pleased as I could be with the case but I was chilled from the cold, damp air. I wished then I had taken time out for Willa's cup of hot coffee. I turned the heater on in the car and we both felt better when we got warm.

We continued on down the road, both of us silent, Charles puffing his pipe, thinking about what had happened that day. Nothing bothered us, not even the broken windshield wiper scraping across the glass.

"Where is this next call?" he finally asked.

"Stormy says to go out the Catlettsburg-Cannonsburg Road to the top of

Bayless Hill. At the very top of the hill, turn sharp left up a steep driveway. He told me the man's name was Wilmer Jones."

Charles, who knew about everybody in the county said, "I don't believe I know him."

We were getting close to Mr. Jones' house. The rain had stopped but it was still bone-piercing damp. I turned off the road at the top of Bayless Hill and drove up the steep drive. As we topped the little hill, I saw a man in the yard holding a kerosene lantern. I had no more than stopped the car and stepped out when Jones came over and grabbed me by the arm and said, "It's about time ya got here." He slurred his words and it didn't take a temperance lady to tell he was staggering drunk. He reeked of liquor and through his slurred talk he added, "My poor cow's bag is about to bust from whar that damned Copperhead bit her." Charles and I overlooked his not too tactful greeting and I told him to take me to the cow.

We went on to a little outbuilding that housed my patient and with the light from my good flashlight and Wilmer's lantern, I examined his cow. Her udder was inflamed, hot and hard. Sure enough it looked like Wilmer said, "it was going to bust." I took her temperature. It was high. She was a very sick cow.

"Snake bit, ain't she, Doc? Just give her a shot of that snake bite stuff you guys use. That'll fix her up—she's a costly brute and I sure cain't afford to lose her."

I stood up from examining the cow's udder and looked over at Jones just as he took a big drink of whiskey from a pint bottle he pulled from his hip pocket! "Mr. Jones, your cow has mastitis. She's not been bit by a snake."

He shook his finger at me and with a sudden outburst, almost shouting, he said, "By Gawd, I think she's snake bit and I want you to give her a shot of that serum. I damned well know when a cow brute's been Copperhead-bit."

I took no offense, realizing he was drunk. I didn't hesitate a minute and I turned to Charles and said, "Hand me a syringe and a bottle of—snake bite serum—out of my medical bag. This cow has to have a shot."

Charles never hesitated and reached into the bag and took out a syringe and the first bottle of medicine he could find. "Doc, here's the snake bite serum and here's the needle. What else do you need?"

I glanced at the bottle of medicine he had given me. It said on the label,

"Vitamin B Complex." I smiled to myself and looked over in the dim light at Charles. He had a grin on his face a mile wide. I filled the syringe and gave Wilmer's cow a great big dose of the medicine. Then I said, "By golly, Mr. Jones, that 'serum' should save her life." Then I put an antibiotic up into her udder and injected her with a dose of penicillin.

Right away he asked, "What's that shot for?"

"Well—that's another shot of snake bite serum. I just wanted to be sure she had enough."

Charles' grin was wider than ever!

"Well, Doc Martin, you guys sure as hell know what you're a doin'. That damned snake could have killed my cow." He stopped talking for just a second or so and reached into his hip pocket and got his bottle of whiskey. "How about us havin' a little drink?" We both declined and then he added, "You'ns don't mind if I have a snort do ya, I'm all shook up over this cow?"

Now I know the cow got well because Wilmer Jones came in to the office a few days later to get some more mastitis medicine. He bragged on how good my snake bite serum was and told me how much he appreciated me coming to see his cow that dark, rainy night. He was still about half-way drunk.

My friend, Charles, and I over the years have discussed many of the farm calls we made together but the we always have a hearty laugh when we remember the case of the snake bit cow.

§   §   §

Sometime later in the year, and after countless numbers of farm visits for different ailing animals, I was up on Bolt's Fork Road at the Prichard place looking at a lame horse. When I was through with my work, I had a nice talk with Mrs. Prichard about our coming here to Kentucky and how satisfied Mary Helen and I were with our region. She thought a minute and then commented, "Doctor, they's goin' to be some big changes in your time. We won't be livin' like this in a few years. I chance to say, there won't be a milk cow or a mule or a work horse any place left in the whole country by the time you are as old as I am." Mrs. Prichard was along in her years, late seventies or maybe her early eighties at this time. "Then what is the likes of you goin' to do for a livin'?" I listened to her with interest and down deep inside me I recognized some truth in her remarks.

When I first moved to the eastern Kentucky, there were seventy-three dairies in my county alone. The surrounding counties, all larger than Boyd, the one we lived in, had as many or more. By the time the mid-fifties arrived, health department regulations and production standards were changing. Dollars dictated the path the small dairy owners followed. They either bought the new equipment, constructed milking parlors and milk processing rooms, the new trend, or went out of business. State and federal health regulations with the constant cattle testing programs for tuberculosis and brucellosis, both diseases transmissible to people, was not easily accepted by many of the not-well-educated-little-farmers. The larger outfits bought the small dairyman's livestock and the little guy was out of business. As the old saying goes, "It takes money to make money."

Most of the dairies were clean, efficient, owner-operated and managed. They were a pleasure to work in. The Highland Dairy Farm, owned by the Crider family, had a herd manager, named Earl Robinette. Earl, a hard-working and dedicated man, managed the cattle while Bill Crider, the farm owner, did the farming. This dairy bottled milk and had a regular delivery route operated by another part of the family. It was a good operation, but eventually it went out of business as the dairy industry changed to more modern large-scale management.

Ernest Bonzo and sons had a big dairy operation in Greenup County. They too bottled and sold their milk locally. Hickory Hill Dairy Farm, owned by Mr. and Mrs. John Evans, was another example of efficiency. This farm was one of my best accounts, and it was not uncommon for me to be there two times a day! Big Garner Creek was a good agricultural area that included not only the Lofty Vanhoose dairy but two McGlothlin dairy farms, the Clyde Ross dairy, Everett Hamilton's operation, and John Henry Klaiber's nice dairy farm on Long Branch, a tributary of Big Garner Creek. Harry Fannin, the Robinettes, and L.C. Caldwell had big dairies on the main highway from Ashland toward Louisa. On the eastern side of the county, Paul Thacker and his brother milked cows up on Durbin Creek, and the Bowling boys had a good operation in the same general area. Closer to Ashland, the Federal Correctional Institution operated a large dairy to supply the inmates with milk and butter. Along with these sizable operations, there were a multitude of smaller, but well operated dairies sprinkled all over the county. And then there were many little not-so-clean operations which operated in spite of constant vigilance by the health department. At the time dairy farming was a major agricultural business in our area. The business was there for a veterinarian, but the huge area and the poor rural road systems created real hardships. I was young and thrived on the hard work, but my automobiles didn't have the stamina I did and had to be replaced every year!

Strict health department control and new operating regulations mandated modern upgraded equipment. The high cost of the new equipment, and its maintenance, nibbled away at the diary farmer's profits, but milk prices were regulated and remained the same. It was obvious this business could not survive. The small operator went out of business first, and then, one by one, the large dairies closed. Today, there is not one single dairy farm in my county!

I recognized that the region, and my career, were bound to change and I constantly looked for new ventures to explore and new ideas. The Martin Veterinary Clinic was a success. More and more trucks parked in my parking lot with ailing cattle, sheep, hogs and horses. The practice was changing but the little, one-cow operations still demanded some of my time.

I began exploring new approaches and new aspects of veterinary medicine.

MOONSHINE

O N A HOT SUMMER AFTERNOON, DURING THE AUGUST "DOG DAYS," George Hobbs brought his dog to the office to get it vaccinated against rabies. He put the dog on my examination table, I filled the syringe and quickly gave the dog the injection. Hobbs chuckled, "Doctor, that's sure a quick way to make money!"

"It sure enough is but it gives us more time to talk." No one else was in the office; time was no factor.

Hobbs was a personable man and we were soon engaged in discussing a recent outbreak of the dreaded rabies disease in our county and the serious- ness of it in our end of the state. "It's a real problem and sooner or later some program will have to be developed to help solve the situation. But until a program is established, it takes people like you to conscientiously have your pets vaccinated every year."

The conversation went on to other things besides rabies.

He told me he was the assistant farm manager at the Federal Correc- tional Institution just south of town. I took advantage of this conversation and asked him about the possibility of getting some work there.

The query brought a flood of information. He began, "I am in charge of the pig and poultry operation. We raise Red Duroc hogs because they are a good meat hog." He went on to explain they had their own brood sows and, "the very best boars we can buy." He continued, "we raise our own pigs and after they are weaned and fed to butchering size, they are slaughtered in our slaughterhouse right there on the farm. The finished products, the hams, bacon and pork chops, go to the mess hall to the inmates." He also told me the poultry department produced all of the eggs and chickens used in the prison mess hall.

"We also operate a sizable dairy. We milk Holstein cows three times a day."

"Three times a day? That's a lot."

"I am sure you think this is an unusual system but it keeps our milk production high and at the same time, keeps the inmates busy. The farm manager is in charge of the dairy. He oversees the milking and maintains a breeding and replacement program for the cattle." He paused, "It's a good operation, but it provides some real headaches."

George Hobbs had a captive audience in me and I asked if they had much veterinary work to do and, if they did, what was the most common problem. "Doctor, our biggest problem comes when the sows cannot deliver their pigs. When this happens, both the sow and her pigs usually die in the birthing process."

"Mr. Hobbs, I am amazed at this statement. I have never seen very many problems that couldn't be solved when sows farrowed. If baby pigs cannot arrive in this world by natural birth, or with a veterinarian's help, it is no problem to do Caesarean operations and deliver the piglets surgically. This is a common procedure and most veterinarians do it routinely."

George Hobbs looked at me with astonishment and said, "Our veterinarian never has mentioned anything like this before or, for that matter, offered any solution to our problem."

I jumped at this opportunity. "I know how to deliver pigs and how to do the surgery if it comes to that." I added I would certainly appreciate the chance to help the next time a sow was in trouble.

This was my first insight to the scope of this operation and right away I asked him about doing all of the veterinary work. He told me the job, like most federal private contracts, was on a yearly bid basis. He added the current contract would expire in January; if I was interested, he would send me a proposal as soon as possible. Before he was out of sight from the office, I had a rough draft of my bid written, ready to be typed and mailed.

In just a few days after this conversation, the phone rang and the caller was George Hobbs. "Dr. Martin, we have a sow in hard labor. Looks to me like she needs your help. I'll meet you at the guard tower across the road from the farm." Almost before he was through talking, I was on my way.

Hobbs met me at the guard tower, waved to the armed guard and told me to follow him. We stopped at a long, low, brick building which was the farrowing house. Inside this building, along each wall, were roomy concrete pens. Each pen opened to an outside area where the sows could exercise or soak up the sun on the cool spring days. A shelf, about a foot from the floor and extending eighteen inches from the wall, was fastened along three sides of the inside pens. These shelves added safety to the baby pigs when their moms lay down. Clean wood shavings covered the floors in every pen. I was amazed at the cleanliness. It was hard not to notice these amenities and right away I made up my mind I was going to be their veterinarian—no matter what!

I went right to work. I admit I made quite an issue of cleaning up the sow, sterilizing my obstetrical instruments, scrubbing my hands and arms and putting on sterilized rubber gloves before examining the sow. I was trying to convince Hobbs that I was a really good doctor. Then after restraining the laboring animal with some hand-held partitions designed for that purpose, I gently inserted my gloved hand into the sow's vagina. Carefully I examined her and told Hobbs and the farm manager, Mr. Havelka, this was a simple farrowing problem, easily solved, "in these days of modern veterinary medicine."

Havelka looked at Hobbs, Hobbs directed his conversation to me and repeated what he had said to me a few days earlier in my office, "We have this trouble all of the time and if the sow can't deliver herself, we lose all of the baby pigs and sometimes the sow too."

My delivery plan was made before I removed my examining hand from inside the sow. I knew this was going to be easy—the gods were certainly shining on me this day! I also knew if all went well with this job, as soon as the present veterinarian's contract was over, I had a new job. I delivered eight healthy baby pigs. Havelka and Hobbs both were amazed at the entire procedure. I didn't reveal one reason the delivery went so well was my small hands made those "inside jobs" easy! It wasn't long before I had a long term contract which lasted until the prison farm was phased out some years later.

George Hobbs was not born a farmer. His knowledge about farm management and the pork industry came from intense reading and observation of similar projects like the one here in our prison. He was an open-minded man and ready to listen to anything that would better his facility. For the record, when I first started working at the FCI, Hobb's pork operation was the poorest in the federal prison system. Pigs died, the wrong kind of hogs were raised, and the slaughterhouse techniques were not the most efficient. He and I together spent hours researching and working on this project. We won. Two years later Hobbs changed his pork production record from the worst to the best! I am proud I was part of the improvement—the program itself.

In the meantime I tried to learn as much about the Federal Correctional Institution as I could. Our goverment operates many of these correctional institutions all over the country. The inmates incarcerated for their offenses were generally from the regions proximate to these establishments. In our case, most, but not all, of the inmates originated in the hills and mountains of Kentucky, Tennessee, West Virginia and the Carolinas. I also learned a small part of the local prison population consisted of tax evaders, a few car thieves and other violators of the federal legal statutes. A large number of the inmates were in there because they refused to pay Uncle Sam taxes on the beverages they made in their own back yard distilleries. In other words, they were moonshiners.

I was on the prison farm every day. If an animal showed the least sign of any discomfort, I was called at once. One day each week Hobbs supervised the hog-slaughter operation and I was called to inspect the meat before it was passed on to the inmate population. It was an ideal place to work, clean and well operated and, with the inmate population, I had plenty of help. I soon had a following of inmates, most of whom were from farm backgrounds. Now, granted, these inmates were not all dumb. They knew if they worked for me, they had an easy job and as long as they were helping me, they were excused from their less glorious prison work. This arrangement was first class and I started teaching my helpers little things that helped me and later, if they ever went back home to their farms, would help them too. Havelka and Hobbs both approved.

You don't discuss the Kentucky Highlands, the people and their culture, for very long until someone smiles and mentions whiskey. To be more exact, homemade whiskey. Most of the homemade whiskey in the hill country is made from corn and is called moonshine, because it was made out of sight, after dark in the light of the moon. This stereotype has always been applied to hill country culture, whether it be Kentucky or some other state.

My introduction to Moonshine and its makin's, as they say here in my region, came directly from moonshiners themselves, experts at the trade—

prisoners at the Federal Correctional Institution. These inmates were serving their time after violating the law by making and selling illegal whiskey. Out of sheer curiosity, after I got to know some of these offenders well, I had long talks with them about their lives and especially how they made their "shine."

One of the inmates, a tall, slender, soft-spoken man named Arnold, was from the mountains of Tennessee. He was a whiskey maker; he had broken the Federal law. Arnold was one of my helpers with the animals, and I got to know him fairly well. He was the major source of my moonshine education. Arnold's family consisted of a wife and six children, his widowed mother and an unmarried sister waiting for him down in the hills of Tennessee. He was a gentle family man with a soft personality that just seemed to grow on you. He spoke often of how much he missed his children.

When I first started working at the prison, daughter Terri was small, maybe five years old. In the summertime she accompanied me on most of my daytime calls. She particularly liked the prison calls because they had newborn piglets, little baby chicks and sometimes young calves. It was a must, every time we visited there, for me to show her around, even let her hold a baby pig or chicken! My friend Arnold befriended her. One day he said, "Doctor, she's jest like my middle aged 'un." After that, when he saw me drive up the road going to the farm, he looked first to see if Terri was with me and if she was, he would get her a baby pig or baby chicken to play with. He soon appointed himself—my baby sitter!

It was a good arrangement. Arnold didn't have to work while I was there, the entertainment didn't cost him anything and Terri, pardon the pun, was in hog heaven! Arnold was my moonshine schoolmaster and I had many conversations with him about "copper worms," "thumper" and "starter" barrels, and other items that make up a distillery or what is commonly called a still.

Now let it be recognized that even the correctional people didn't consider the whiskey people criminals like the thieves and other felons in their institution. The illegal distiller was there because he didn't conform to the law of permits and pay the taxes associated with the manufacture of alcoholic spirits. What they knew they learned from their fathers and their grandfather before them! Matter of fact, there was a lot of sympathy toward these people because while they served their time in jail, their families were having hard times and very little income. Not too many thought makin' 'shine was a wicked crime. Consequently, as long as Arnold and my small daughter were not out of sight, there was little concern about the arrangement.

One day I needed some extra help with a cow trying to deliver a calf, and the farm manager directed a fellow they called Red to help me. In the course of my labor, and my small talk with the inmates, I mentioned I liked to hunt ruffed grouse—a wild bird indigenous to the rough land we lived in. Red spoke up and said, "Doctor, we got more of them old wood's pheasnants on my place than we have chickens. You're sure welcome to hunt 'em there any time you want to." I soon learned his "wood's pheasnants" term was common where he came from.

"Where you come from, Red?"

"Just back of Olive Hill a piece, about four miles. Got a little place on Sinkin' Creek."

Olive Hill, Kentucky, is about thirty miles from Ashland in Carter County. A great deal of Carter County is rough hill land but it is blessed with a lot of natural beauty such as "Sinkin' Creek," Carter Caves, some large man-made lakes, high rock walls and deep hollows. Sinking Creek got its name from the geography. It meandered along and then it disappeared into the side of the hill only to surface again a few miles away. Someone prophesied the Garden of Eden was really in Carter County! But whatever, it was Red's home and was generally a good source of inmates for the FCI, most of them moonshiners.

"Thanks, Red, maybe some day I'll take you up on that, but I'll wait 'till you get home."

"Your welcome any time. I'll tell m' boy you be comin'." I inquired about Red and was informed he was a "whiskey man" and was serving time for his sins!

Arnold made his usual visit to me one day and inquired about my daughter, who by this time was going to school and didn't come with me on my calls while school was in session. "Doc, I'm a goin' home in two weeks. I done done my time." His Tennessee drawl emphasized his excitement.

"Arnold, we've been friends for some time now. I appreciate your good help and your befriending my daughter. I surely wish you well." After I thought a while I said, "I don't ever want to see you back here again."

I didn't see Arnold anymore. One day I asked George Hobbs what ever happened to him, as I hoped he was back in Tennessee with his family. I got the surprise of my life when Hobbs told me about Arnold.

"Doctor, he was supposed to be out of here two weeks ago. He was to walk out on a Monday morning. Well, Sir, on Saturday he didn't show up for the afternoon head count. He was missing and so were two other inmates. A search found all three of them up behind the hog feedlot drunk as they could be!" He stopped to light his pipe and then went on, "The three of them had been taking a little sugar, spoonful at a time, and some fruit each day from the mess hall and with this and a little still they rigged up, had been making whiskey for some time—right here on the prison farm! Well, Sir, they were all drunk and right now they are over inside the institution paying for their escapades." Arnold was released about a month later and I heard no more from my friend.

Bird dogs and shotguns were one of my weaknesses and with these tools during bird hunting season, I tramped the hills in quest of that woodland bird, the grouse. One evening a hunting friend of mine called and wanted to know if I wanted to go to Carter County and grouse hunt on the "prettiest piece of land I have ever walked on." Curious about his remark, and anxious to pursue my favorite sport, I accepted his invitation.

We drove out to Olive Hill and in the middle of the little town turned off and drove a few miles into the hills. Bob, my hunting partner, showed me where to go and pointing ahead to a little house tucked up in a hollow, told me to pull in there and stop. At the same time he said, "You better stay in the car. I know these people but sometimes they don't take kindly to strangers." I sat in the car while he walked up the path to the house and knocked on the door.

After a brief conversation, Bob and the farmer walked to the car. Bob introduced me and, to my utter surprise, I was welcomed like a long lost friend! My new acquaintance told me he had been expecting me for a long time and even added he was disappointed I had not been to visit him sooner. I was perplexed at this welcome for a moment. Then he told me his daddy's name was Red—the same Red I knew in the federal prison! Red had told his family about me on one of their weekly prison visits. His boy's name was Mike.

Bob was certainly correct; this was truly a beautiful place to hunt. The farm was nestled along the banks of a small stream that meandered through a valley completely surrounded by high rock cliffs. The valley floor was covered in knee deep green grass. Summer's wildflowers still bloomed in warm places that gathered the sun. Big oaks and huge fir trees that had never seen a woodsman's axe added to the awe-inspring quality of this place. This was virgin timber, impossible to haul up the steep rock walls and out of the valley. The creek, edged with sandy banks, had deep pools with fish big enough to be fisherman's prizes. Meandering along without rhyme or reason, the creek suddenly disappeared into the side of a rock wall, lost for a while but to resurface a few miles away. This was Red's "Sinkin' Creek."

Bob and I hunted there for several years, never tiring of the beauty and wildness of the valley. When we first went there, Mike asked us not to hunt on one part of the farm. We respected his hospitality and didn't question why he didn't want us there. We were pleased we had this hunter's paradise all to ourselves. Up on the high ground, above the creek was a different story. There was evidence, nearly every place you looked, of a big moonshine operation. There were large piles of broken Mason Jars and bashed-in fifty-five gallon barrels, once used as cookers for the corn mash. The cool waters of the creek cooled the coils and was used to dilute the mash. It had been an ideal place to make liquor. But sooner or later the Alcohol, Tax and Firearms people, characterized as "revenuers," did their work well and Red went to jail.

One evening after a hard day's hunt, I made it back to the farmhouse before Bob decided to call it a day. His old dog, Duke, was working a running bird and Bob was determined to follow it and maybe get a shot.

Mike met me as I walked out of the woods and while we waited for Bob, we sat down on a log out by his stock barn and talked about a cow he had bought at the Catlettsburg Stock Yard. The conversation soon drifted from the cow to his dad and then to the day's hunt. It was just sociable kind of talk only two men would enjoy.

"Doc Martin, you want a drink of some good whiskey?"

"Mike, that doesn't sound like a bad idea at all." I knew he was talking about 'shine. I don't really like corn liquor but it would not have been the thing to do to refuse this gesture of friendship.

He got up from the log and walked about thirty feet to a turnip and potato patch, pulled up a shovel that was stuck upright in the dirt and started to dig. Two shovels full of dirt revealed a fruit jar full of crystal clear whiskey.

Nestled in a row next to it were several more jars of whiskey. I never said a word, realizing our out-of-bounds area was where the cookers were at work making whiskey!

Bob eventually got back. He found the grouse and missed it when it roared out of the woods. He had a taste of the liquor too, and thanking our host and leaving our best wishes to him and his family, we drove back home.

§   §   §

On more than one occasion, when Mary Helen and I woke up in the mornings, there would be gifts at our front door left by our rural friends. Sometimes we found vegetables when they were in season; on more than one occasion there were chickens dressed and ready for the skillet. One time the doorbell rang and one of my clients handed Mary Helen four squirrels just freshly dressed. He said, "Ma'am, these was killed this morning just at sunup. The Doctor's been awful good to us, and my wife and I thought you would like some fresh meat."

I had another farmer, and a really true friend, named Sable Tabor, at Olive Hill. One day Sable and I were talking and the subject came up about corn whiskey. He said, "Do you like that stuff?" I told him if I had another choice, I would take the other choice! He smiled and agreed with me that you sometimes had to be a hardy soul to drink some of it. Sable drove an old black Chevrolet panel truck with two big speaker horns mounted on the roof. He was in the movie theater business and advertised his shows weekly by driving through the rural areas blasting the still countryside with news of the coming features. One morning Mary Helen and I were jolted out of our sleep by a booming voice of Sable's sound truck telling us to look on out front porch, he had left a present. That he did, he left me two one-gallon jugs of whiskey. There was a note attached to one of them, it said, "Don't drink what's in this jug. It's for your friends. The other jug is pretty good stuff." It was signed, "S.T."

Homemade whiskey was never hard to find in our country and most everybody knew where you could get it. Rumor has it that most of the prominent businessmen in our county began their successful ways making or buying and selling bootleg whiskey.

§   §   §

One evening just before closing time in my office, John Irwin, County Extension Agent in Greenup County, called and asked if I could come and look at a sick mule. The mule was on a farm way back off the main road, and if I could meet him in Greenup town, he would go with me on the call.

It was late when I met John but the darkness was tempered by the light of a full moon. We drove several miles out into the county and eventually turned off of the main road to a graveled county road and followed it for about a half mile. Then we crossed a creek at a shallow crossing place and drove another two miles to the foot of a big hill.

"Stop the car, but leave the headlights on. You sit here and wait. I have to talk to somebody."

I never moved a muscle. I did exactly like he told me to do. In the darkness of the night, I was completely confused. While he was getting out of my car, I looked around, full of apprehension, not knowing what was coming next. Looking up toward the top of the hill I could vaguely see by the bright moonlight, several men standing in the road in front of a pickup truck. John Irwin stepped out into the beam of my headlights and waved to the men and shouted out his name. He told whoever he was talking to he had the doctor with him. The lights from the truck flashed on and off briefly and John got back into the car. He then explained the men on top of the hill were moving whiskey and he had been warned when the call about the mule came in, to be on the lookout for them and identify himself when we got to the foot of the hill. I was relieved. This was better than going to the movies! We went on, passed the men and their truck and I treated the mule. On our way back, there was no evidence of men or the truck. Their mission was completed as was ours. I made a little money and I assumed they did too.

Now, all of this moonshine business doesn't have much to do with veterinary medicine but, nevertheless, at that time it was—and I guess, still is—a part of the hill country culture. In turn, I became part of this culture when I moved to Kentucky and worked for the people and shared some of their everyday experiences. There were many other incidents that involved making whiskey and some involved me. Bootleg whiskey was easy to get but after our county was voted wet, which allowed whiskey to be sold, the moonshiner retreated to areas where theirs was the only source for the drinker. I am sure though, someplace in Boyd, Greenup, Lewis, Carter or Elliot counties, and for that matter the other mountain counties, someone is still making 'shine. It wouldn't surprise me either if some younger Arnold, or perhaps another Red, with their smuggled sugar and mess hall fruit, didn't have a hidden cooker behind the prison hog lot. Frankly, I don't condone this, but I can't help but wish them well as they continue the liquoring traditions of the hill country.

HYDROPHOBIA IN THE HILLS

G EORGE HOBB'S VISIT TO HAVE HIS DOG VACCINATED AGAINST RABIES
ultimately led to my contract at the Federal Correctional Institution. I am grateful for that and I am also grateful for people like him who
religiously vaccinated their animals in our constant battle against rabies.

Hydrophobia, a misnomer for rabies, has been a dreaded term ever since
man knew there was such a disease. Mr. Webster's dictionary, describing the
word hydrophobia, in part says, ". . . a dreaded fear of water." That's inaccu-
rate. These infected animals are not afraid of water but simply cannot drink
because most rabies cases involve a paralysis of the lower jaw. But no matter
what you call it, rabies or hydrophobia, it spreads fear through the heart of
man. There is no cure; once infected—the patient always dies!

In the mid-nineteen hundreds, rabies was a persistent problem in the
thinly populated area of the hill country. Feral animals—(wild dogs and
cats without owners), skunks, foxes and raccoons—were the vectors that
spread the disease. Hardly a week went by when I didn't see at least one
rabid dog or cat.

The symptoms divided the disease into two distinct phases. The first was
the aggressive, snapping and biting "mad dog" time. The second was the
late stage of the disease where the paralysis sets in and the animal eventually dies. We call this the "dumb" form of rabies. But, no matter what the
symptoms indicate, it is the same disease. I had no choice but to admit these
sick animals into my office, wait for them to die then have a laboratory
examination of the brain tissue to confirm my diagnosis. I was never wrong.

When a case of rabies was diagnosed, the local health departments quar-
antined the area for a month. No dogs were allowed to roam free until the
fright was over. Ironically, nothing was ever said in those days about cats, a

dangerous reservoir for the virus. Blaring signs were posted on the telephone poles, and the newspapers published the notices, and the radio and television stations spread the word as a public service.

Concerned citizens met with the health authorities and eventually with the city and county elected officials. I attended many of these meetings, urging political support mainly with an animal control system. Our pleas were heard by the county officials, but the answer always came out the same. "We don't fool with a Kentucky man's dog." They contended their job was to build roads and increase the tax structure and make our county a better place for the citizens. They didn't have time or the money to build control shelters and monitor the animal population. What they didn't say was when you fool with a man's dog, you lose a vote. Their political position and desires overshadowed dog control and was not a politically healthy move. I made enemies with more than one local official as I pleaded for support.

Now, nearly fifty years after the fact, the state law requires every Kentucky county to have some sort of an animal control system. Not all counties have conformed! The politics and a self-serving system is still there.

Eventually the voice of the people demanded some sort of a control program. The veterinarians and the residents together established temporary clinics in every community. The fee for vaccination was lowered and the people came. Hundreds and hundreds of dogs and cats were vaccinated; many had never felt a hypodermic needle before. Everybody participated and the disease was eventually managed. Periodic rabies vaccination as the result of these programs became a part of the animal owner's routine.

These community projects worked very well, and later, as the health departments became involved, rabies was nearly eliminated. The effort was so successful, I doubt if the young veterinarians of today have ever seen a clinical case of "hydrophobia." I hope they never do.

§   §   §

We hadn't lived in Ashland very long until I had my first personal brush with the disease. One evening a lady came into the office with a short-haired black cat. It was a big cat, glaring at me through huge, yellow eyes.

"Doctor, my cat's different," the woman said. "She avoids me and this morning I found her hiding in a dark corner of my pantry." She paused a moment. "To tell the truth, I am afraid of her." I looked at the cat and something in the back of my mind advised caution. I managed to take the animal's temperature. It was high. The apprehensive owner was not surprised when I told her I thought the cat might have rabies. Then I carefully picked her cat up and just as carefully put it in one of my new steel cages. I told my client I would call her and keep her informed as to the cat's progress.

The next morning my horse trainer friend, Pidge, came to the office to discuss a horse we were treating in his barn. Before he left I mentioned the cat and he wanted to look at it. I obliged. We went to the kennel room and I explained the cat's symptoms as we looked at the animal through the bars of the cage. The cat had turned over his water pan and the cage was, besides being soaking wet, covered with spilled cat litter and waste from the cat box. I asked Pidge if he would clean the cage if I would hold the cat. He agreed after I assured him I would not let the cat loose.

I put on a pair of heavy gloves and carefully reached into the cage and caught the cat by the back of the neck. Pidge did his job while demanding, "Doc, you be damned sure you got a good hold!"

Cage cleaned, I guided my frightened patient back through the open cage door. Quicker than a snake can strike, it happened—the cat twisted itself from my hands and sank its teeth into my hand! Even through the gloves it hurt. Suddenly I was in a near state of shock. Pidge was frantic. He kept saying, "Oh my God, oh my God, oh my God." Then, "Let me get you to the doctor."

"No, not yet. Let me sit down and get myself together, but first I have to clean this wound." I went to the sink and washed the bite wounds with surgical soap and encouraged them to bleed freely, hoping the blood would wash away the infected saliva. "I'll call Dr. Stone's office and see what he has to say about this and if he wants me right away, you can drive me up there."

I called my MD friend and told him about the accident. He suggested I stop by his office, which was only a half block from my house, on my way home and he would have some vaccine ready. I thanked Pidge for his concern and sent him back to his horse barn.

Harry Stone's waiting room was full of patients waiting to see him, but his receptionist ushered me immediately to one of the examining rooms. After finishing with a patient, he came into the room and looked at my chewed up hand. He asked me if the cat was truly rabid and I assured him it was.

"Well," Dr. Stone was a talker, "I have the vaccine and I will give you the first dose now." He nodded to Vivian, his nurse, and she filled a syringe with vaccine from a small bottle. "Frankly, there is no use for you to come here every day for a shot, I'll give you the vaccine and you can give it to yourself. This will save us both some time." Vivian gave the injection and handed me the vial with the remaining vaccine. He started to walk out of the room to his next patient but stopped and said, "If you have any headaches or other side effects, come see me."

"Wait a minute, where in my body should I give myself these shots?"

He laughed, "Just any place you can reach—a different place every day." Then he was gone, I left his office for home, full of anxiety, mainly concerned about the effects the vaccine sometimes had on patients.

My hand was red and sore the next day and I soaked it in hot water twice before it was time for me to give myself the first injection. I figured Harry had given me the first one about five o'clock the evening before and I would continue on that schedule until all twenty of the remaining doses were gone. I sent Curtis, my helper, home just at five. I filled my syringe with vaccine, swabbed an area on my arm clean with alcohol and, gritting my teeth, winced as I injected the medicine into my muscle. Each day I repeated this ordeal and was getting along fine. About the sixth or seventh evening I had just injected myself when I looked up and saw my neighbor standing in the doorway quietly staring at me. I am sure he thought I was some sort of a dope addict and before he could say anything, I quickly told him what was going on. He admitted he had seen me "shoot" myself the night before and, on his wife's insistence, had come to investigate! After that episode, I was never really sure if those people were friends or foes. In three weeks I used all of the vaccine on myself. I was not mad with the disease, but mad at myself for being so careless. It never happened to me again.

§   §   §

Once an outbreak of rabies started, I got busier, especially in the farming areas. In the Big Garner Creek section where there were several dairy farms, everyone but one man lost at least one cow to the disease. Hampton McGlothlin had his entire herd of Guernsey cows vaccinated. He paid a high fee for those times, but was a winner when his herd stayed rabies-free. All of the farmers along Garner Creek had their dogs and cats vaccinated. Temporarily we had that area protected.

§   §   §

Alan Ross was a county commissioner. He was also on the committee who enticed me to come to Boyd County. One day Alan called and told me he had some steers, "acting crazy." He said, "Bet you a buck, Doc, they have rabies." I didn't take his bet because I was sure he was right. I drove up the lane to his farm and there penned in a tight corral were two steers, absolutely in prime condition. They were good enough to be show stock! Outward appearance revealed two normal animals, nothing unusual about their behavior. Questioning Alan about his animals I found out his hired man, Manley Hulett, shot two foxes in the pasture about a month prior to this visit.

Manley, who was standing there with us, interrupted the conversation and said, "Doc, them old foxes jest didn't act right. They wasn't scared or nothin'. I shot one of 'em and tha other one jest hunkered down. I killed it too. I knowed then they wuz mad." Manley was right; those foxes had to be rabid and they no doubt were the cause of these steers being infected. I explained to Alan and Manley most cattle and horses got their bite in the face and nose as they grazed in the fields where the rabid animals would lie and wait.

Ross asked me if I was sure his steers had the disease. I told him not really, but I would give them a test. I turned to Manley and asked him to, "go get me a light-colored chicken."

"What's that fer?"

Alan spoke in a soft, but very demanding, voice. "Manley, do what Doc said—this is serious business." Manley went to the chicken house and in a few minutes, still wondering what I was up to, came back with a big white rooster.

Everything was ready but Alan and Manley were still uncertain what a white rooster had to do with their steers. "Manley, toss that old rooster in the pen with those steers and let's see what happens." Manley looked at me, then back at Alan Ross. Alan nodded and Manley tossed the big flapping rooster into the corral. The sudden flash of white movement immediately aggravated the steers, and they both bellowed and tried to attack the bird! The rooster, unhurt, frantically flapping its wings and cackling, flew its way out of the pen to the safety of the barnyard. My simple test proved my point. I was convinced the steers were rabid; Alan and Manley were too.

"What do we do now, Doctor?"

"Destroy them and if you want, I'll send their heads to the state laboratory and confirm this diagnosis."

"I respect your knowledge, no need for the extra expense."

I shot both steers with a twenty-two caliber pistol. A single bullet dropped each animal. The case was closed.

§   §   §

About a mile from the lane where you turned to go to the Ross farm, the Rankin family had a country store filling station restaurant combination. This was a community gathering place, the center of activity for all of the farmers. Mrs. Rankin, Nora, operated the restaurant. She knew my taste preferences and, over the years, fed me very well when I stopped there on my daily rounds to the farms. Her husband and children worked the store and filling station. They also had some cattle, and I was their veterinarian. When the rabies outbreaks flared up, such as the one at the Ross farm just a mile or two away, they advertised vaccination clinics with signs on their store windows and by word of mouth. These clinics did very well, and for several years I went there and vaccinated cats and dogs. The people in this area, like those on Big Garner Creek, took the matter into their hands, bypassing the county officials and their reluctance to be involved in this public health issue. Up until now, there was no organized controlled program to eliminate this situation. Together the locals and I did what we could to fight a disease centuries old. Together, and later with the state's aid, we eventually won. In retrospect, I truly believe my involvement in rabies control in this hill country gave me more personal satisfaction than anything else I did. I truly served my community.

§   §   §

Many in other areas shared the same fate. Some lost horses, and quite a few had hogs die with rabies. Believe me, a hog with rabies is an aggressive animal.

I saw one old boar, already mean to start with, just south of Greenup, Kentucky. Greenup is a nice little town nestled at the confluence of the Little Sandy and Ohio Rivers. This area, too, was one of my significant practice areas. Tom Phillips was one of my good clients and lived just a short way from the Little Sandy on a small farm. Tom was waiting for me when I opened my office one morning and told me he had a boar, "that wasn't acting just right. Doc Martin, this old boar stands and shoves his head against the walls of the hog lot like he damned near has a headache! Another thing, he jumps and flinches at the slightest movement." We both agreed the boar probably had rabies but Tom wanted me to look at the animal. "Doctor, if you can come sometime this morning, I'll stay home from work and wait on you."

I finished my office work and drove to Greenup town, turned left and followed the Little Sandy River Road to the turnoff to Tom's house. It was a modest farm. He raised a few pigs, a flock of chickens, a garden and a house full of kids.

There had to be eight or nine runny-nosed little humans waiting when I drove into the barn lot. All but one of them was shy. All of them, except the bold one, turned and ran to the house. This was a little girl about nine or ten years old. She was bare-footed, had her hair braided into a pig-tail, and looked like she hadn't had a bath in a month. She came running up to me just as I was getting out of the car and wanted to know my name, and what I was doing there! Tom told her, "Go away, Cynthia, leave the man alone." Cynthia never budged until I told her who I was and what I was going to do. She insisted she carry my medical bag, and right away, I knew I had a new helper.

The hog lot was constructed with slab boards, the bark still attached. It was a good stout pen, and like most of them, it was a quagmire of mud, filth, flies and smells. Nailed over the top of the pen in one corner was a piece of old galvanized roofing that offered some shade to a hog on a hot day.

This boar must have weighed four hundred pounds. He was a big Duroc and had a set of tusks that would have made any razorback hog envious! The boar was standing just like Tom said, with his head pressed hard against the sides of the pen. Like Tom, I imagined he must have a headache. I surveyed the situation for a few moments and then little Cynthia said, "Mister, watch what happens when I poke this old hog with a stick." Before Tom or I realized what she said, she sure enough jabbed the boar with a long stick and all hell broke loose! The boar slashed at the boards with his teeth and banged headlong into the side of the pen. He rumbled horrible noises and threw his head from side to side, flinging mud and saliva in every direction. He snapped those huge jaws and awesome teeth at everything, real or imaginary. In his final move he bit down on one of the pine slabs and crushed it to pieces. The power of the deranged sick boar was almost beyond belief. For a moment there was complete silence. I looked up. The last I saw of my helper, Cynthia, was a fleeting glance as she ran through the front door of her house to safety. There was no doubt the boar was rabid and on my advice he was destroyed.

§   §   §

These are just a few of my personal experiences but other veterinarians shared similar situations. The widespread problem with rabies was not limited to my state, Kentucky, but was epidemic in neighboring southern Ohio and western West Virginia as well. To those of us in the veterinary profession it was frightening. It was obvious something had to be done besides the individual and small local community efforts to establish clinics.

About two years after I opened my practice, the Kentucky State Legislature, urged on by the severity of the disease and the insistence of the state Department of Health, was presented with a bill proposing all dogs be vaccinated against rabies every year. Once again the request was bucked by the politicians who repeated, "You don't fool with a Kentucky man's dog." Eventually the bill was passed and became law, but only after heavy lobbying by the drug manufacturers. I am sure with their lobbying, the manufacturers interest was self-serving as well as public spirited!

Now there was a tool big enough and strong enough to get the job done. The local health departments, with the help of the Kentucky Department of Health, went all-out planning and advertising the proposed clinics and explaining how they would work. The plan was for the health departments to establish the time and place and to advertise for each clinic. They also agreed to furnish clerical help needed to issue certificates and keep the needed records. The vaccine was administered by the local veterinarians at a reduced fee. The plan worked.

§   §   §

My first scheduled clinic was held in Olive Hill, a small hill country town big in the timber business in years gone past. Its main claim now is limestone which is quarried and shipped over most of the eastern part of the state for roads, driveways, building stones and field lime. The town is in Carter County, a typical rugged hill country area. In preparation for these clinics I optimistically ordered two thousand doses of anti-rabies vaccine. I had a firm commitment from the drug company stating I could return what I didn't use. The clinic at Olive Hill was scheduled to begin at nine o'clock in the morning at the playground of the local school.

I arrived there to find mobs of people, trucks, cars and kids gathered for what appeared to be a big celebration. There were dogs tied to car bumpers and tied to trees. Pickup trucks and flat-bedded trucks had dogs tied in every corner and believe it or not, in these modern times there were two horse-drawn wagons full of dogs on the scene! There were dogs confined in all sorts of crates and cages and to create more confusion, some dogs were just running loose! There were big dogs, little dogs and medium-sized dogs. There were pretty dogs and ugly dogs along with mean dogs and even meaner dogs. I saw very few timid, shy little dogs. This day they were all giants and all were adding to the turmoil and confusion. The voices of the people, trying to overcome the din of the constant barking, added to the carnival atmosphere! I wondered, surveying this horde of dogs and people, if I would have enough vaccine. It would be disaster to run out at this stage of the game and face the wrath of those left out. I dispatched one of my helpers to Grayson, the other town of size in Carter County, to borrow extra vaccine from Dr. Rodney Gross, my veterinarian friend in that town.

The health department people did their job well. They had tables set up forming a rectangle with ten or twelve ladies waiting to help. The regimen was for the animal-owner to go to the table, register his dog, pay the fee—a dollar and a half in those days—get his certificate and rabies tag and then come to me and I would administer the vaccine.

Besides this being a public effort for the good of everybody, it was also sort of a social gathering. For every dog on the premise there had to be an entire family. The kids had their dogs and their parents and, sometimes, their grandparents too! It developed into absolute chaos. The lines of people at the registration tables stretched from the school building back to and down the street. Days later, some person who was there estimated there were over three thousand people in the gathering that day! There were dog fights. There was one man fight when one person accused another of having stolen his dog. Dogs urinated on trees, on the legs of the clerk's tables and on each other. I watched one man stand oblivious to a large fox hound hiking his leg and soaking the owner's pant leg while he was talking to his neighbor! The celebration, if you want to call it that, got wilder and the local policeman had to take away a few who were celebrating the "day of the dogs" with a product of their own making, clear corn whiskey.

The lady who directed the clerks soon saw there would be a lot of money change hands over the tables and she periodically collected the money and put it into the school safe. Now keep in mind, these were good, hardworking country people who earned their living from the fruits of the land. Many did not understand what the vaccine would do and, believe it or not, some had no belief in it. They came only because it was now the law. Some disbelievers figured out how to beat the game. They simply paid their money, got the tag and certificate and went back home without the vaccination! It didn't take long to realize this was happening and later, at other clinics, we changed the registration procedure and the owner didn't get the rabies tag until they presented the certificate to me, and I gave the injection. Nevertheless, in spite of those few dissenters, over ninety percent of the dogs were vaccinated that day.

I was busy. I did have foresight enough to take one of my office helpers with me, and his job was to fill the syringes and keep my work-table top clean and disinfected. I injected the vaccine as soon as the dog was put on the table, trying to make way for the cleanup and the next animal. It didn't take long to inject the medicine—one man who looked away just as I vaccinated the dog, declared I had cheated him and not given the shot. The person standing in the line behind him assured the irate one I had given the injection. No persuasion satisfied him. To settle the issue, I gave the dog another dose of rabies vaccine.

Somehow I managed to have enough vaccine and suddenly realized I would need to order more for the next clinic which was scheduled a week later at another location. By the day's end, my fingers were sore from pushing the plunger of the syringe. When the last dog was vaccinated, and everybody thanked for their help and cooperation, the lady who had collected the money and I went into the schoolhouse to tally the results. We estimated we had vaccinated just over seventeen hundred dogs that day! She had the money done up in bundles with a rubber band around each bundle. The loose change was in a bank sack, and altogether, the receipts came to nearly three thousand dollars! This was more money than I had ever seen in my entire lifetime! In my mind, this also created a problem, since there were maybe three thousand people there that day who knew there was a lot of money involved. The lady clerk and I put the wads of paper money in a lady's dress box and while no one was looking, shoved it under the seat of my car. Needless to say I was apprehensive all of the forty miles back to Ashland. I stopped at my house just long enough to call the local FBI agent and asked him if he would be so kind as to park my money in his safe until I could get to the bank in the morning. He agreed and that ended my day at Olive Hill.

Other clinics were created—bizarre things happened at them too. One case I well remember concerned a man and his dog at a clinic in the rural community of Kehough, a village in Greenup County. This man had a beautiful English Setter. The dog was striking in appearance and his owner was fast to tell me his dog was as good a hunter as he was good-looking. We talked a while, and after he loaded the dog into the back of the pickup truck, he waved at me as a gesture of our mutual feelings about this fine hunting dog. The next day I had a phone call from this man and he informed me on his way home his dog tried to jump out of the truck and was dragged by his chain under the wheels and was killed. I felt almost a personal loss too. This was a nice dog and a compassionate man.

The clinics continued all that summer and were scheduled again for the next year. The veterinarians involved made suggestions to help: the main one was to include cats in the program. This suggestion was never incorporated into the law, but cat fanciers realized the risks too and more and more cats were vaccinated at each clinic. These clinics continue to this day, although not on as large a scale as in the early days. Most people learned it was easier to pay the regular fee in the veterinarian's office and avoid the hassle of long lines, dog fights and inconvenience.

In a matter of two years from the beginning of these mass immunization programs, there was a noticeable decrease in the incidence of this horrible disease. Clinical cases of rabies disappeared, and the threat to livestock and the pet industry as well as human death and suffering had been nearly eliminated.

Reminiscing, I believe I can truly say I have seen as many clinical cases of rabies as any veterinarian my same age, except those that live in this area and went through the same times. If I never see another case I will be completely content. I applaud the veterinary profession, the health department officials and most of all the citizens, for their concentrated efforts to make this improvement in public health possible.

SOCIALIZED MEDICINE,
MY KIND OR MAN KIND

W HEN PEOPLE-DOCTORS, THE "MAN KIND," GATHER, THE SUBJECT OF SO-cialized medicine invariably comes up. It certainly bears consideration and for both human and animal medicine.

Many physicians would lead you to believe the idea of socialized medicine or, correctly, government-directed medicine is like a cancer to their profession, destructive and undesirable. It is my belief that most of these practitioners have been brainwashed by a few that are more self-serving than compassionate. Those few fear losing insurance payment money and reduction of sometimes exorbitant fees and the fear that their man-made halos will be forever turned off! But, believe it or not, these doctors—the very ones that are raising all the stink about it—are already practicing in this controlled invironment. Cases in point: Medicare, Medicaid, and support of Veteran's Administration facilities. Surprisingly enough, those gripers are blessed—and they know it—because they have many pluses from this system.

In my kind of medicine most DVMs serve as their own internists, surgeons, radiologists, pharmacists, dentists and bill collectors. They also become adept at building management, painting and plumbing and are occasionally shocked when they try to fix bad wiring in their own buildings. They do this out of necessity because most "vets" can't afford many of those luxuries. The physicians, as a rule, have specialists that do this for them, operate in public facilities and if something breaks, just buy a new one and pass the bill on to the consumer, in this case, the patient. I should say this has been true for the last fifty years and still holds true for most non-city veterinarians. In the last few years, however, some big-city clinics and high-powered veterinary practices have created animal treatment facilities which rival human hospitals. Some still do not. Am I angry? Am I jealous? No, I am just telling the facts as I see them.

Now that I have that off of my chest, I certainly support the compassionate, caring, well-trained MDs and DOs that take care of the populace. Like every barrel of apples, there are far more good ones than the proverbial rotten apple.

Socialized medicine in human medicine has in many cases been a blessing not only for the patient but for the doctors involved. Again, as a case in point, public health clinics, the military services and other state-federal facilities treat sick people at public expense. In cases like this, they cannot deny it is good.

Socialized medicine has for years played a big part in veterinary medicine. It has been a prime tool in controlling the major animal-human disease factors such as tuberculosis, brucellosis and rabies. These programs, even though they are dictated by government agencies, do not interfere with, or invade, the private practice.

Tuberculosis, or "TB" as it is commonly called, was fairly prevalent in poor areas and particularly in the hill country of Ohio, West Virginia and Kentucky. The disease is transmitted from animal to man, man to man and from animal to animal. Most people are aware of this disease that infected so many people and caused much suffering and death. Until the middle part of the twentieth century no effective drugs were available to cure or prevent TB. The sick died at home or were sent to a sanitarium in a better climate—all in hopes they would get well.

Brucellosis, known by most of the farmers as Bang's disease, caused abortions in young cows and poor production and unthriftiness in older cattle. The disease is also endemic to sheep, goats, swine and dogs and—frightening enough, people! In humans the disease is called undulant fever. It is transmitted to people through byproducts of the infected animals such as uncooked meat. It is a chronic, debilitating disease suffered by many butchers, veterinarians and farm people who handle infected cattle and hogs. Until just recently, there was no known cure and the treatments today are far from specific.

As we have shown, rabies is a horrible disease that has been around since the beginning of mankind. It is incurable and always fatal in man and beast. The veterinarians and their mass vaccination clinics, in reality a form of socialized medicine, licked this disease.

There are other diseases too, such as hog cholera, a certain strain of equine infectious anemia and constantly-occurring mutant viral infections that are under regulatory control. Even though hog cholera and the horse viruses don't make people physically sick, their monetary losses are upsetting. I guess being broke, by the loss of their cash crops, is to some people almost as bad as being physically ill.

The livestock industry and farmers managed to survive in spite of these diseases, while suffering heavy financial losses as well as sometimes suffering devastating illnesses. Eventually, through the cooperation of the state and federal agencies, programs were developed and funded by the government that led to elimination of these problems. But, it didn't come without long hours of hard work and personal sacrifice on the part of everybody involved.

The regulatory agencies established programs. To be qualified to participate in these programs, only those veterinarians accredited by the federal government were qualified to participate.

When Mrs. Prichard on Bolt's Fork said to me, "Doctor, they's goin' to be big changes in your time." I agreed. Then when she added, "Then what's the likes of you goin' to do for a livin'?" I listened. Her prediction was coming true. I had no choice but to participate in these new programs if my profession was to meet the changing times and my personal future was to be secure.

§   §   §

Just after World War I was over, our federal government established the first big animal disease control program, its ultimate goal to get rid of the threat of tuberculosis being passed from animals to humans. Nearly every farm veterinarian was asked to participate and most responded. Some veterinarians did nothing but TB testing, going from farm to farm every day. The United States Department of Agriculture furnished the tuberculin, the test agent used for their skin tests, and paid the doctor a small fee per head for cattle tested. Through the Depression years of the twenties and thirties, this program's meager dollars kept many veterinarians from financial distress.

The program went on for years. The veterinarian would inject the tuberculin into the cow's skin and seventy-two hours later return to the farm and look for reactions. If the injection site was inflamed, the animal was branded on its jaw with the letters "TB" and was sent straight to slaughter. The farmer received compensation for his losses. Year after year this was done but it seemed there was never an end to the problem. The disease seemed to crop up in spite of the test and slaughter program. Realizing other animals might be involved, testing later was broadened to include hogs, sheep and goats.

Eventually testing, and new drugs for treating the disease in humans, resulted in a semblance of control. Most of the public tuberculosis hospitals were closed and the country went on about its business. In spite of the success of this program, testing is still done and now that the twenty-first century is just a few years away, documented cases of tuberculosis are still found. Newer medicines are effecting a cure in most cases. Some strains of the disease are still resistant to treatment.

While the tuberculosis program was under way, brucellosis—the cause of man's ailment, undulant fever—went uncontrolled. Out of the public health need and partially because of the success of the TB testing, the United States Department of Agriculture developed a government-subsidized program to fight this disease.

§   §   §

Brucellosis, or Bang's disease, as it was named as a credit to Doctor Bang, the scientist who isolated the bacterium that cause the disease, was common all over the world and "Bang's" testing was routine when I first started to practice. Cattle going from one state to another or being exhibited at fairs or livestock shows had to have health certificates indicating they were TB and Bang's free. People like Henri Riekert, Paul Pollitt, Troy Fairchild, Everett Fannin and the 4-H Club kids that exhibited their cattle in our area were all aware of this requirement. Of course producing dairies were required to have annual TB and Bang's tests. These people presented no problems.

The brucellosis testing program cost the farmer nothing and the veterinarian was paid by the state. The only stipulation by the officials was for the owners to participate freely. Most did; some never did! Every bovine breeding animal was tested. Of course steers, sexually neutered animals raised for beef only, were exempt. Testing was done from a blood sample taken from each animal. Participating veterinarians drew blood and the sample was shipped to a testing laboratory for final diagnosis. If, as in the TB program, the animal proved to have the disease, it was branded with a hot iron on its jaw, in this case with a "B." The reactor was sent to slaughter and the owner was paid a fee for his condemned cow. Since I was the "large animal vet" in our area, I was selected to direct the program in this region. The veterinary colleges were contacted and students were given the opportunity to work under the supervision of the doctor. This program, started in 1960, gave them some hands-on work as well as some cash in their pockets. I had three interns working for me the summer of the program.

Every morning I gathered my neophyte veterinarians together and told them whose herds I had scheduled for testing. Then I sent them on their way to draw blood samples from each animal. At the day's end, the students brought the samples and associated paperwork back to my clinic for processing and shipment to the laboratory for testing. In a matter of a few days the test results were back, the owner informed of his herd status and the reactors taken care of, if there were any. Some herds were disease-free and needed no more testing for a year. The infected herds were subject to repeated testing until they cleared up. It was hard work but it made a little money, got you close to the client and created either good will—or got you into trouble as the case could be.

Hill people found it hard to accept the fact our government was controlling their lives more and more every day, so compulsary medicine was suspect among them.

This was truly socialized medicine of the positive kind, and some of these situations made for an interesting day!

The Programs and The Problems

Testing cattle for Bang's disease was hard, sometimes dirty, and always physically difficult work. Under certain circumstances it was also very trying and upsetting! The easiest situations were in dairy barns, where the cattle were secured in stanchions, or the beef cattle operations which used holding chutes. The one-or-two-cow owner with no holding facilities was the hardest situation, as it generally ended in some sort of wrestling match between man and beast! Personalities and lack of understanding could play a part too.

§ § §

H.P. Thrasher was one of my interns. He was just over five feet tall, and close to that around around the middle. He was the oldest of the three interns; Richard Featherston and Jim Sousley were the other two DVMs-to-be. All three were students from Auburn University. All three eventually became good veterinary practitioners, and I like to think my presence and their time spent with me was part of their education.

One morning Mr. Thrasher left the office to test his cows per the schedule I had set up the previous day. He called me from a country grocery store telephone and informed me that his cow owner on Bolt's Fork refused to let him bleed his cows. Matter of fact, he told my man in no uncertain terms he wasn't going to let anybody, ". . . test 'em or stick a needle in their hides!" Thrasher also told me the man said, ". . . to git," and, "Dr. Martin, I did." I told him to go on to his next appointment and I would talk to the farmer and try to reason with him. The next morning I went to the man's farm and I was given the same ultimatum, "Git off'n my property." Like Thrasher, I did.

I called the sheriff and in a few days I bled those cows under the protective eyes of the law. There were no reactor cattle in this herd, and the owner finally came to his senses and reluctantly helped spread the word to cooperate and get the cattle tested.

Most of the work went smoothly. Thrasher's experience was an exception, but all of us had at least one similar experience associated with the program.

§   §   §

My appointment was with Mr. Chris who owned a small dairy in Greenup County. I was scheduled there at seven o'clock. I arrived on time, and as I drove down the lane to the dairy barn, I noticed the cows were up on top of the hill grazing. What was this? They were supposed to be in the stanchions waiting for me. I stopped at the milk house where my client, leaning up against the side of the building, watched me drive in. He never said a word. I got out of the car, took the test tubes and rack, needles, lariat, clipboard and other things I needed and after uttering a disgusted "Hello," walked into the barn. There was one cow fastened in the stanchions. I looked at Mr. Chris, he looked back at me with a sheepish grin on his face and before he could say anything, I asked him, "How come your cows aren't here?"

Chris was a sleazy little guy, not very clean and had a habit of looking away from you when he talked. Glancing down at his feet and kicking something imaginary out of the way, he told me in his own sort of a way, "Doc, I think this is all bullshit but since I am a real civic-minded citizen," he paused to let his rhetoric impress me, "I agreed to participate." His attitude didn't surprise me. Twice before I experienced dealings with him and both times I had a feeling I had been toyed with. He was an agitator. I knew he had a scheme of some sort on his mind, but I still couldn't figure out why there was only one cow in the barn.

He raised his head and looked at me out of the corner of his eye, but before he spoke, he shifted a large chew of tobacco from one cheek to the other and spit a big stream of tobacco juice toward the floor. "Hell, Doc, git smart. Jest fill your bottles up with blood from this here cow brute. I know she's OK 'cause I just bought her at the stockyard and you tested her there just a couple of weeks ago."

I didn't "git smart" like he suggested, packed my gear and put him on my list of dissenters. Later on, after the sheriff talked to him, I did go back, again under the protection of the badge, and tested all of the cattle. My cow owner was nowhere around to face me personally, but instead had his hired man there to help with the work.

For truth's sake, Chris was not this man's real name, but I am using another name to protect myself because the owner is still alive and still is a trouble-maker.

§   §   §

On another occasion I went to a farm to brand a reactor cow. Before I left my office I phoned the farmer and I told him to put the cow in the barn and I would stop on my rounds and brand her. Sure enough, the cow was tied up when I got there. I plugged my electric branding iron into an electric outlet in the milk house to get it hot while I checked the ear tag number to verify I had the correct animal. I looked at the ear tag and then I knew I had been tricked. Instead of a nice big Holstein cow who was the real reactor, the farmer substituted a thin, nondescript dry cow that wasn't worth feeding! She had the same ear tag number as the reactor, but the tag had been switched from the sick cow to this one. How did I know the animals had been switched? Just by chance, intern Featherston, when he bled the herd, made an unusual note on the chart. He wrote, "This cow's got white circles around her eyes like she wears glasses!" Why he made that notation I will never know but it revealed a fraud. This cow had a solid black face. Rather than get into a fuss with the owner, I turned this herd over to the state supervisor under the pretext there was mistake made in the records. The state official re-bled the herd and eventually the real infected cow was removed from the herd.

§   §   §

John Klaiber out on Big Garner Creek called and wanted his herd tested some evening after he milked. Doing it this way gave the cows time to settle down and be back in full production at the morning milking. This was not an unusual request by the dairy farmer. John milked about forty cows in a good, concreted, airy and spotlessly clean barn. Twenty stanchions filled the milk parlor; the cows were fastened in these stanchions facing a wooden wall that separated the milk room from the main barn. This unusual arrangement left only thirty inches of space between the cows' heads and the wall. It was a tight place to work.

John Henry, as he was called by his friends, was a tough, slender, wiry individual who never knew when to stop working. He kept his fences repaired and his buildings in good shape. Like most every farmer, he wore bib overalls and knee-high rubber boots. His checkbook and a penny pencil were always ready in the bib of his overalls. Mrs. Elsie Klaiber, his wife, was a jovial lady who was a career schoolteacher in the area schoolhouse at the mouth of Big Garner Creek. She ruled the house while John at least thought he was lord and master over the farm. Both were willing to accept changes and both cooperated when it came to farm problems and decisions, always trying to find something better for the future. Elsie even volunteered to "keep the records," when we bled the cows. I thanked her but it was not necessary.

The milking was over and I bled the first twenty cows with no problems. John turned the first bunch out and I had about half of the second group bled. There were seven more to test. John caught the next cow, a nervous heifer, with the nose lead and pulled her head around to the side so I could get to her jugular vein and to give me room to work in the narrow space between the cow and the wall. I stooped down in front of her and jabbed the needle into her vein. With a bellow so loud you could hear her at the next farm, she lunged forward and knocked me down. As she reared up, her back legs slipped out from under her and she fell on top of me! I was in a lot of pain. My ankle was badly hurt, possibly even broken.

Hurt or not, over the objections of John Henry, I managed to test the remainder of the herd and somehow I managed to drive back to town. The pain was severe and I knew if I ever took my boot off, I would not be able to go at all and I still had one more call to make. For this call I had to go over the river into Ohio to tend a sick horse. By chance a drug salesman friend of mine came to the office to tell me about some new medical items and volunteered to drive me to my next patient. He and I together treated the horse, then he drove me back to my house.

I took the boot off when I got home and just knew I had a broken bone. Sure enough, the next day x-rays confirmed my diagnosis and I spent the rest of the winter hobbling through my chores in a walking plaster of paris cast! This is not quite the end of this story. As the weather grew colder and the winter snows and rains came, it got harder and harder to keep my foot clean since my outside office was generally a barnyard. Mary Helen solved my problem, with a plastic garbage bag held up with a garter of Scotch Tape over my plaster cast.

§   §   §

There were other painful experiences, and I must relate just one more. I was at the C.E. Fannin Blue Ribbon Farm to test his herd of horned Herefords. This was a good herd consisting of outstanding show stock animals. They were well cared for and pampered as no other cows in our county were. I was on this farm frequently and often knowing what was to be done, just went ahead and did the work by myself. Fannin's barn was an old dairy barn that still had double rows of stanchions in place. Mr. Fannin and his helpers fed these animals in the head yokes and they were no trouble to catch.

When I got to the barn there wasn't a soul around. It made no difference, I knew my help would be there shortly so I went ahead, caught the first cow with the nose tongs, tied her head around to the side and drew my blood sample. It was no problem, but without help, and with the handicap of my plaster cast and broken foot, it took longer. Over the years I developed a habit of not numbering the test tubes. I kept track of them by systematically putting them in the test tube rack the same way in the same sequence every day.

There were seventy head of big, fat, good-looking horned Herefords waiting for my service. I bled just shy of forty by myself while I was waiting for Fannin's hired man to come and help me. I set the test tube rack with my blood samples up on a window sill out of the way and, as I moved down the line of cows, I moved the rack on to the next window. I had just finished bleeding a big cow and turned around to put the tube in the rack when my helper came in. I did not see him or hear him as he came up behind me and said, "Hey Doc, sorry I'm late . . ." He startled me and as I turned around, I hit the test tube rack full of blood samples and spilled them all over the floor! Only a few broke but since they were not numbered, I had no way of knowing which sample belonged to which cow!

I must have looked like I was shot and I am sure the oath I let out was heard clear up the road. I did manage, "You startled me when you . . . "

My helper never let me finish. "Damn it, I'm really sorry I scared you and caused all of this mess." He could say no more and I knew it hadn't been an intentional thing. But the damage was done and with his help I re-bled the entire herd. You can bet your last cent, this time every sample tube was numbered with a grease pencil. From that day on, it was standard procedure.

It had not been a good day at all. Besides losing the blood samples, I was out of garbage bags to cover my cast and in the struggle to do all of the work myself, had waded through pile after pile of warm fresh cow manure. It seemed that nearly all of it found its way under the cast all the way up to my knee! When I got home I took the garden hose and squirted water under the cast and washed it out the best I could. That didn't work. I made my decision. With my pocket knife and the help of an electrician's wire cutter, I chopped and whittled and finally got the cast off. Gingerly I tried to put some weight on my foot and found with a little discomfort, I could walk on it. Then, to finish the job, I treated my foot and leg to the first good bath they had seen in two months. I never went back to the doctor. The cast was never put back on.

The testing program continued all summer and through the remainder of the year. My interns returned to their studies, and, with the help of some lay bleeders the state sent to me, we finished testing our area. It had been a rewarding job and eventually the area was declared "Bang's Free." In a few years the entire United States would approach that status but never did we see a truly Bang's free country.

Like the physicians, I am not a true advocate of socialized medicine but in the brucellosis program it did the job.

CATLETTSBURG STOCKYARD

THE LEVISA FORK AND THE TUG FORK RIVERS MEANDER THROUGH THE mountains of eastern Kentucky and eventually meet at Fort Gay, West Virginia, and its neighboring town, Louisa in Kentucky. The union of these two waters then becomes the Big Sandy River. The Tug originates in the rugged mountain country known locally as The Breaks of Sandy. The Tug Fork and the Big Sandy River form the eastern boundary line between Kentucky and West Virginia. To the west of this area the Russell Fork and Beaver Creek come together at Allen to form the Levisa Fork. This river system is the life blood of eastern Kentucky and flows through the very heart of Appalachia, offering the path of least resistance from the mountains of Kentucky and West Virginia north to the Ohio River valley.

This watershed and its tributaries are steeped in history, folklore and superstitions. The area is the source of millions of dollars in coal and timber. It also serves as a pathway for many tired of the rigors of mountain life or, for those with visions of fortunes in their mind, to seek new areas of endeavor. In the early years the good and the bad migrated downstream to where the Big Sandy empties into the Ohio River at Catlettsburg, Kentucky.

Catlettsburg itself is steeped in history and can recall Civil War days, the timber boom, and huge rafts of logs floated from the mountains to their doorstep. There were the boisterous days of saloons, river boats, gambling and drinking brought on by the speculators from upriver towards Pittsburgh and the adventurers from the hill country who came looking for their fortunes. Livestock owners, or drovers as they were called, walked their animals from "up Sandy" to the Catlettsburg stock pens and sold them to the highest bidder who then shipped them by boat to Cincinnati and Pittsburgh. In time the timber industry faded and the steamboats docked for the last time. Coal was now king and the railroads laid their tracks to the coal fields to haul out the real gold of our land. But the livestock industry survived and old timers still recount stories about, "tradin' days at the livestock pens."

These older citizens tell me all kind of tales about the stock pens in Catlettsburg, the spirited auctions and the antics of the traders and farmers. One retired farmer, known to be a real storyteller, delighted in telling me it was a ". . . whiskey-drinkin', cussin', 'backer chewin' and sometimes a fightin' affair." He told me they traded hogs, cattle, knives, guns and dogs; discussed politics; bought, sold and traded for land; discussed the price of livestock and the merits of a good woman. From his conversation, he seemed to cover it all. When the "tradin'" day was over and the stock pens empty, they walked back home, some many miles away.

The stock pens as they were called in those days are still there, and soon after I came to Kentucky I was employed by the Catlettsburg Livestock Sales Company as their veterinarian. It was not their doing, but rather the federal and state governments required a veterinarian be at each sale. My job was to test the cattle going back to the farms as breeding stock for Bang's Disease and to vaccinate pigs against hog cholera. On occasion I castrated a bull or a horse, dehorned a long-horned cow or gave an antibiotic to prevent some infectious disease. On animals going from our state to another, I examined, tested the animal and issued a health certificate attesting to its status. It was just like the old-timer told me, only not nearly so boisterous or glamorous!

My stock yard at that time was old and the buildings were not in the best repair. The roofs leaked, the buildings were often dilapidated, drafty and dirty in spite of the constant attention by the employees. I soon realized it was the coldest place in the world to work in the winter and I couldn't imagine Hell being any hotter during the summer months. The work was hard, no place for the weak or timid! But the reward was fairly lucrative and, Lord knows, during those times every dollar counted. In some of the newer, more modern establishments the sales ring was air conditioned or had big electric fans for the buyers' and sellers' comfort. Catlettsburg yard had no air conditioning but two big fans stirred up the dust, odors and flies in the sales ring. The auctioneer brought his own electric fan and directed the cooling air toward himself as he sang his chant; the customers sweated, some fanning themselves with hand-fans—free advertising from the local mortuary.

Working there was like being in another world and spawned many stories: some good, some bad, some happy, some sad. For twenty five years the
stockyard was part of my life.

§   §   §

My business office, if you could call it that, was a table in the aisleway of
the small office where the lady clerks collected the money from the buyers
and paid off the livestock sellers. I tested my blood samples and made out
the required health certificates at that table. At no time when I was working in this office did I have any privacy or sense of being part of the business.
On the other hand, in the stock pens I was the king. I got along well with
the men, and what I said concerning the health of the animals was absolute
law. I represented Kentucky's Department of Agriculture and enforced their
rules.

I held court in a working area, which I helped design. It was located
midway along the side of the sales barn next to the railroad tracks. My domain consisted of a small holding pen and a catch chute, a larger pen where
I turned my cattle into after they were sampled and eight or ten hog pens.
Between the hog pens and my test pen was a steep loading chute used for
moving cattle and veal calves into railroad cars for shipment to the East
Coast markets. Part of the test pen itself and most of the pig pens were
under this ramp. Many times when I was bleeding cattle or vaccinating pigs,
the yard men would drive cattle up the ramp into the waiting railroad cars,
never once thinking about the urine and the manure and other filth that
filtered down on "Doc" Martin. After the bare necessities were installed, I
insisted on a wooden wall being built between the test pen and the alley
alongside the railroad tracks. This was intended to keep out the wind, hot
sun, rain, the wintertime snow, and the dirt and smoke from the passing
trains. The carpenter who did the work, in his haste to get the work done,
left two-inch cracks between the boards. I complained to the owners and
they said the carpenter told them the cracks were for ventilation. I can tell
you for certain when the snows came and the wind howled, it was surely
well-ventilated! Finally I had a catch chute built to hold the cattle when I
worked on them. It was made of railroad ties and heavy timbers, and after it
was done, one farmer commented, "Doc, that chute is strong enough to

hold an ox." Pun or not, he was right!

It was routine to bleed the animal, open a gate on the side of the chute and drive the cow, or the bull, out of the holding chute into another pen out of the way. It was not unusual to bleed fifty to seventy-five head of cattle a day. I also vaccinated pigs against hog cholera. The more pigs there were in those small, dusty pens under the loading chute, the better I liked it. The more pigs, the more money I made. All in all, it was a pretty good deal. I counted on the stockyard income each week to feed me and my family and pay the help and expenses of the clinic.

Stockyards are notorious for their personalities and my yard was no different. Since this story is really about the people here in the hills, it would be unforgivable if I didn't tell about some of them.

§   §   §

Everett Fannin, the man who owned Blue Ribbon Farms and the local bus company, showed up every sale day dressed in his stylish business suit, never minding the flecks of manure and the mud that often splashed on him. He always came by the test pen for a social talk and to pay what he owed me. One day when he stopped by, I was short of cash and I asked him if he remembered the bill I sent him for some work I had done two months previously. He thought a minute and said, "I know I wrote that check, but for the life of me I don't remember mailing it. I'll tend to it when I get back to the office." He left but was back in about fifteen minutes with a torn dirty piece of paper that proved to be my check. "Doctor, I found this on the floor of my car with a lot of other checks. I guess I'll have to take care of them too." As the years went on, I frequently asked him for my money and he always paid, but I was amazed that such a successful businessman handled his affairs like that.

§   §   §

"Boo" Rice was the sheriff. He owned a good farm out south of Catlettsburg and grazed several head of cattle. Like clock work, his law enforcing duties ended at stock-sale time and didn't resume until he sold his cows or bought some new ones. Like so many people of the area, each endeavor had its priorities!

§   §   §

Many of the customers at the stockyards were professional traders. They spent their days going from market to market, buying here, selling there, operating on a small profit or loss margin. In a week's time their trucks could be seen in the parking lots of most of the sales barns within a hundred-mile radius of Catlettsburg. The good traders were generally successful and for a small fee bought and sold cattle for their farmer friends.

Wick was a trader. He was a likable little man, poor but energetic. He was also a pen hooker. A pen hooker is a trader who runs and meets each truck before it gets to the loading dock and tries to buy the animals before the auction at their own price. They gambled on buying low and selling what they bought higher through the sales ring. Most of the sellers ignored them. Wick wasn't the most successful trader in the bunch. He had a reputation for buying sick, cheap animals at other sales and bringing them to Catlettsburg for resale. He was determined to make a nickel with something, regardless of the consequences. Most of his animals were hard lookers, unthrifty and many nearly at death's door! When he brought them into the market each week I faced him, and every week, he would vow he wasn't aware of their poor health. After my talk to him he would just smile and say, "Shucks, Doc, I won't bring no more sick 'uns." Come next sale day Wick would back his truck up the truck dock and look to be sure I wasn't around before he unloaded his not-so-well livestock for the day!

§   §   §

Ova Diamond was one of my good friends and a small dairy operator I had for a client. He lived on Big Garner Creek along with the McGlothlins, John Henry Klaiber, the Vanhooses, Dick Brogan, Everett Hamilton and Clyde Ross and his family. He was also a serious cow trader and attended every sale. Ova, and I don't mean to be really critical, was lazy. I'll never forget driving by his farm one day on my way to the market. Ova had his stock truck parked at the barn, loaded with trading cattle. He was sitting on the porch drinking a glass of cold, fresh milk. He was absolutely content. Ova's young son, Jimmy, was standing in the road, hands on his hips, the perfect image of a younger Ova, watching his mother hoe the weeds out of the garden!

One very hot day, the temperature was up in the nineties, Ova came by my test pen where I was vaccinating some calves and said, "Doc, let's you and me go across the street and I'll treat you to a cold beer." I never hesitated, put down my syringes and climbed over the high fence and walked with him across the street to the beer joint. The place was full of cow traders and other stock men cooling down in the wonderful, seventy-degree air-conditioned room. It felt really good and after three big schooners of ice cold beer, the cool atmosphere felt even better. Well, Ova and I finally gave up on the beer and started back across the street to my test pen and then I realized I had too much and was about halfway drunk! Of course we recovered, but Ova's wife found out about our escapade and we both got a stinging lecture directly from her.

§   §   §

During that real hot spell, a chewing tobacco salesman came to the market and passed out free packages of Mail Pouch. Naturally I took one because it was free. I never chewed before but since most of my farmer friends did, I figured I would give it a try. I stuck the package in my hip pocket and went back to testing cows. Between animals I decided to try a chew. I opened the sack, took out a big wad, just like I had seen my friends do, and crammed it in my mouth. I bit down on it and it only took two or three chomps on that stuff until I gagged. I thought this was the most horrible thing I ever tasted! I spit and spit and spit trying to get that stuff out of my mouth. My stomach was revolting and I nearly got sick. After getting rid of the oversized chew, I finally recovered and vowed to myself never again.

Frank Hatten lived across the Big Sandy River in West Virginia. He and his family ran a first-class dairy operation with which I was proud to be associated. The entire Hatten family befriended me, and we never let a chance to visit get away. Frank always came back to the test pen on sale day just to visit and see if I needed or wanted anything his family could supply or to discuss my kind of business and his dairy.

On the same day the Mail Pouch chewing tobacco salesman was there, Frank came up to the outside of my pen and asked if I wanted something cold to drink. He said he was going across the railroad tracks to the ice cream store and get a milkshake. The thought of that cold milkshake, just after that devastating experience with the chewing tobacco, just seemed to hit the spot and I said, "Yea, Frank, I'll take one just like yours." I went on with my work and in a short time Frank called over the fence and announced he had my cold drink. I stopped my work and reached for the milkshake.

"It's strawberry, I hope it's all right with you."

Just as Frank handed me my strawberry milk shake, he switched his extra big chew of Mail Pouch from one cheek to the other, turned and spit a big stream of amber toward the railroad tracks and without a moment's hesitation, put his drink to his mouth and gulped it straight down! Suddenly strawberry milk shakes became repulsive. I gagged and threw up all over the test pen! You can bet your life I had vowed right, I never touched "chewin' 'backer" again.

§   §   §

The stockyard was also a gathering place for friends and was used on sales day to transact other business besides buying and selling animals. Outside of the sale barn, following the same pattern of earlier years, housewares were sold, and horses and mules were traded along with pocket knives, hound dogs and farm equipment. The years had changed the gatherings very little, and the merits of women were still a major discussion topic. Sometimes the farmer would take advantage of the market's facilities and use them as if they were his own. This was OK with the Bowlings, the owners of the stockyard, because it created good will, and good will translated into more customers. One incident I remember very well as it came to my favorite subject— horses.

Thurston Hurt lived "up Sandy" on a beautiful Big Sandy River bottom farm at a place on the mapped marked, "Zelda." To my knowledge, the Hurt family was all there was to Zelda and where the name came from, unless it was named for a railroad switch site, I do not know. One day Mr. Hurt called and asked me what I knew about buying wild horses right off of the ranges of government land in the West. I told him I knew they were available. I also told him what I read about them indicated they were wild animals, tough and mean. Then he told me he thought he would buy some, bring them back to Kentucky and sell them for what they would bring. He asked me if I would help, since I was his regular veterinarian and had a "passion for horses." I agreed to do what I could.

Some weeks later Hurt called long distance from Nevada and informed me he was on his way home with a load of mustangs. He asked if I would make arrangements with Harold Bowling, one of the yard owners, to unload the horses and hold them there temporarily. Three days later I met Thurston as he pulled his big stock truck crammed full of wild horses up to the dock. While we walked around the truck, and he was telling me what he had done, we talked about what we had to do. First of all, they had to rest, get their fill of good water and hay. Then he wanted them all to have an injection of antibiotics to prevent any respiratory diseases they might have been exposed to in the long truck trip from the West.

The problem was immediate. Up until these animals had been driven into corrals in Nevada, no one had ever touched them. To approach them from the ground would be suicide. I suggested we unload them, herd them down the aisles of the stockyard and crowd as many as we could into my small test pen. The idea sounded plausible and we did just that. Without very much effort on our part, the trip-weary mustangs found themselves packed in my holding pen like sardines. So far, so good. The next step was to figure a way to give them the shots. I decided to work them like I would hard-handling cattle when I vaccinated them. I climbed up on the high fence surrounding the horses and as each rump came my way, I jabbed it full of penicillin. Thurston, standing on the fence beside me, reached down and marked each treated horse with livestock marking crayon. Before long we had all thirty of the horses treated and marked. Then we turned them into my big holding pen, where they had access to some good hay and water. They stayed in the pen for a few days and made an amazing recovery from the long hard trip. We never lost a horse or had what appeared to be a sick one! For sure, the mustang is a tough critter. In time he sold every one of these animals to people that had patience to handle and break them. It worked out well, Hurt made money and the new owners proudly displayed their real wild-west mustangs bought at a good price.

§ § §

When the old storyteller told me about the early days of of the stock pens, he described the ". . . the cussin' and the 'backer chewin' . . . ," activities and then he said that when all was done the farmer walked home. Some lived long distances from their farms.

There were many older people who came to the stockyard on sales day, some to do business, some just to be sociable. The automobile carried people home these days but there were still a few who walked. One was Katy Wilcox. Katy was, as far as I know, a widow woman who lived on a farm up Campbell Branch, a tributary of the Big Sandy River. She was a tiny lady, in her late seventies at the time. Her farm was at least six or seven miles from the stockyard. When she had business there, she would hire a trucker to get her animal to market or deliver a new one home, and then, instead of riding, walked to the market. When she concluded her business, she walked back home! She obviously was a good animal person, feeding her steers by herself, selling and buying just as well as any man.

One evening about five o'clock, I finished my work and started home. It was a cold, damp fall day, not really fit to be outside. It was the kind of a day intended for people to stay home and, like some would say, "set by the fire." I drove up the highway toward home and I saw Katy, walking stick in hand, trudging along beside the road, oblivious to the rain and the traffic. I stopped my car and told her I would take her home. She got in, thanked me and said, "Doctor, you needn't have stopped for me. It ain't very far to the house." By my estimate, the house was still five miles away!

Katie was really a symbol of the hill people. She was strong physically, good of heart and made her own way. She didn't bother anybody and asked for no help from anyone. When I got to her place she thanked me and we became friends. She lived in a big, old farmhouse that no doubt could tell all kind of stories. I could see through the windows the nice furniture inside but she never invited me in. Her thanks for the ride was enough in her mind to cement our friendship. As the years went by, I would occasionally see her walking along the road and give her a lift. She was always appreciative.

§ § §

Of course not everything went well and sooner or later, as the saying goes, "the one you are the nicest to is usually the first one to bite." And bite it did.

Like the Bang's testing, hog cholera vaccination was compulsory. No breeding-type pig could cross the state line without proper health certificates indicating the pigs had been ear-tagged for identification and vaccinated against cholera. One buyer came all the way from northern Ohio each week to buy pigs. He bought them here in Kentucky at a lower price and sold them to the grain farmers who converted their corn into pork chops and hams. Over a long period of time I vaccinated a lot of pigs for this man. One day he came back to my test pen and asked if I would note the amount of anti-hog cholera serum I gave each animal on the health certificate. I obliged him but failed to indicate I was using a new concentrated serum that was just available on the market. It was just a week later when this little pig buyer was back and with him was a Federal Livestock Inspector. They both accused me of malpractice. The buyer demanded all of his money back he had spent for the pigs he said were improperly vaccinated. The inspector, siding with the pig man, showed me the proper dosage for serum in his rule book. I argued the point, mentioning the concentrated antiserum but he retaliated and said I did not indicate on the health certificates that it was concentrate! I was in violation of the law. They both told me they intended to bring a law suit against me if I didn't pay off. The inspector, his crony standing by his side, said I was not only liable for the cost of the pigs but was likely to lose my license. It was a mess.

I was really upset. The pigs had indeed been treated properly and had strong protection against cholera. Finally, not knowing what else to do, I called my insurance agent. They told me to do nothing until they investigated the case. I worried and fretted for several days. The insurance man called me a few days later and told me their investigation revealed these two men had used this very same ruse on other veterinarians and it took my situation to break it up. I was exonerated, the Federal Inspector and the unscrupulous buyer were both convicted of extortion based on another similar case in Ohio. I am sure situations like this, even though I was guilty of nothing, aged me beyond my years!

§   §   §

I continued to work for the Catlettsburg Livestock Sales Company and the Bowlings for several years. A lot of unusual things happened, some funny, some sad. Most were rewarding. But for some reason the friction between the front office help and me continued to grow. To the best of my knowledge, I never offended any of them. I simply think that the office help was jealous because I made more money than they did. One night, after some confrontation with one of the ladies, I blew it all and quit. It had been a wonderful period in my life doing what I really like best, doctoring farm animals. Over that period of time I made a multitude of friends, bought and sold a lot of my own cattle and indeed served my area well.

The Bowlings were good people, good farmers and business shrewd. They knew the tricks of the livestock industry and knew how to make money. They were, over the years, always good to me and helped me establish a good practice. I held no animosity toward them. It was simply time to go to other things. The Bowlings still remain my friends.

§　　　　　§　　　　　§

That evening I told my wife what I had done. She was jubilant and told me she wondered how much longer I could take the emotional and physical strain that went with that job. My old back injury still plagued me, at times making it impossible for me to work. We discussed the changing times and changing economy which was affecting the large animal practice. Again remembering Mrs. Prichard predicting, "Doctor, ther's going to be some changes in your time," Mary Helen and I made the decision for me to give up the large animal practice. It would be hard to give up something that had served me so well for many years. I advertised there would be no more farm work but for a while I still did the horse work.

THE HORSE DOCTOR

*H*e's no better than a horse doctor IS A DISPARAGING REMARK UTTERED AT times by someone about some physician's abilities. I take offense at this statement. It is degrading to both honorable professions. Today's horse doctors are specialists in their field, dedicated to the welfare of the equine animals, the owners and the horse industry. These practitioners are generally far better diagnosticians than most physicians and beyond a doubt, far more compassionate toward their patient and its owner! I am proud I earned the title and was respected as—a horse doctor.

By the end of the 1950s, the Martin Veterinary Clinic was well established. The idea of ailing large animals coming to the hospital was working. My association with the saddle horse people encouraged a good horse practice that eventually spread beyond the local horse area to all of eastern Kentucky, the Blue Grass area around Lexington, West Virginia and Ohio! I was proud of this. I bought a small farm south of town with the intentions of building a horse farm and possibly expanding my veterinary services, especially the horse work, to this property. The land I chose joined my friend Henri Riekert's farm which was on the north side and by the Chris Crank property on the south side. As a matter of fact, I can look out of my window and see the Crank barn, where I broke my back in the early days of my practice! We built a house, a large saddle horse barn and an equipment building for the tractor and other tools. Between the house and the barns we built a small lake and stocked it with fish. Then I surrounded the entire acreage with black board fences. It looked great. We were impressed as were others including the tax assessor who at once raised the property taxes! As a final touch of what we thought was class, we named it "JOMAR," of course, Jo for John, Mar for Mary Helen. We were young, enthusiastic and looked

145

to a bright future. Many unusual things happened during these years and these happenings and the people involved deserve attention.

§　　　　　　　§　　　　　　　§

First let me tell you about my own horses and the farm. This sets the stage for the years to come and my experiences as a horse doctor. Back in the early fifties, Pidge Mohr did his job well with the three-year-old gelding I bought from Reverend Fugate. But at some point in my horse's training, his learning suddenly stopped, and I had a horse that refused to get any smarter. During the course of this training program, another horse enthusiast and I rented the barn Mohr operated and started our own boarding and training stable with Pidge Mohr as the trainer. We were convinced we could make a small fortune in this business, since there were so many horse lovers in our area. In a short time we had our eyes opened about this venture. When we invested a large fortune in the business, it soon became a small one! The horse business, at least from that angle, was not too lucrative. My partner in this barn venture owned a nice, big gelding which he and his wife showed in the harness horse classes at the local shows. We often went with them, and soon the horse show became a sort of a passion with us.

Now not quite so poor, and with visions of eventually making more money, my horse show urge became stronger and I vowed some day I would own a really good horse to show myself. The opportunity came when my brother's wife, Norma, wanted to sell a three-gaited horse she had been showing. She was too busy raising her children and had no time for the horse. I bought this horse. He was well bred, well broken and a very capable gelding. His show name was Heart's Desire, and he and my sister-in-law won many championships together. Norma called this horse Rabbit, and Rabbit he was until the day we eventually sold him. Now that I had a real show horse, I sold the pretty gelding I bought from Preacher Fugate and was proud of my trading ability, realizing a grand profit on this sale of ten dollars! Of course this doesn't consider the hay and grain I had invested which had to be considerable!

Several judges liked Rabbit for his style and previous reputation. Of course we followed these judges and continued to win trophies, ribbons and prize money. We went to a different horse show each week and sometimes made more money with Rabbit's earnings than we did working in my hospital. This was the start of what developed into a very good horse practice, a start-from-scratch horse farm, Jomar, and an outstanding stable of American Saddle Horses.

In the meantime, Terri met the neighboring Bustetter kids who had a brown and white spotted pony that pulled a little sulky. This tiny animal was outstanding and looked just exactly like a miniature horse with fine features and a bit of elegance not seen in most Shetlands. These junior horsemen drove their pony to our house every day and took my daughter for a ride. Terri surely had her daddy's genes when it came to the horses and she at once fell in love with this animal. Never forgetting my childhood desire for a pony, I approached the children's mother about buying her animal. She told me her kids were outgrowing Tonto, the pony's name. Still, she said, the only way she would part with it was for me to find a larger pony of equal value and make a trade. I searched and inquired and finally my mother, who was a schoolteacher in a small southern Ohio community, found a big-ger pony that was almost a ringer in color and manners as Tonto! I went to look at this animal, bought it and left a deposit of twenty dollars in good faith until I could get back with a horse trailer and collect my new purchase. Included in this deal—for all of one hundred and ten dollars—was a four wheeled pony buggy, a saddle and a bridle, a set of driving harness and some spare leather harness parts! I eventually sold the buggy to a man who worked at the steel mill, sold the harness to a man that needed it for a small mule and traded even for Tonto. After we made the horse trade, Mrs. Bustetter volunteered the information that this pony had been imported from En-gland and was listed as a "miniature horse" on the bill of lading. This majes-tic little animal was the second good horse that came to us. This later proved to be the best horse trade I ever made.

Lynn Genius was the name of the five-gaited mare I bought to round out our show stable. She was a lovely horse with exceptional ability. These three horses advertised my presence and the name of "Jomar Farm, a division of the Martin Veterinary Clinic," became well known in the tri-state area.

§   §   §

Over the years the show stable did well and we owned many good horses, but the pony Tonto was the one animal who deserves to be mentioned in this story.

Pidge and I soon realized that properly shod, Terri's new pony could be quite stylish and we started to groom him for the showring. Fancy as he was, he needed a fancy name. After some thought, he was named The Clinic Orderly. With a custom-made show buggy, we toured the circuit for several years and never once were we out of the money! Terri and Tonto made show-ring history together. One day we were showing at a county fair in southern Ohio and The Clinic Orderly had just been judged as the grand champion harness show pony. Terri came driving out of the ring all smiles, blue ribbon clenched in her teeth. She was truly a little six-year-old princess in all of her glory! Dale McDavid was one of my young friends who had attached himself to our stable. He held the pony by his bridle while I helped Terri down from the buggy. Dale went on to the barn with his pony. I started to follow but was interrupted by a man who approached me and asked, "Are you Dr. Martin?"

"Yes sir, I am." I glanced toward Dale who was expecting me to help him with the chores. "What can I do for you?"

In what I imagined an eastern accent he asked, "What will you take for your pony? Give me the bottom dollar."

Proud as punch of Terri and Tonto and just bolstered by another championship, I wasn't even thinking of selling. "Sorry, mister, this pony is not for sale." He thanked me, uttered something like he hoped I would have a nice day and walked away. For some reason I hesitated, turned around and watched him as he got in a big fancy car with an older lady. They drove away in spite of the fact the show wasn't over. I wondered why they were leaving but it didn't take long to get the complete answer.

No sooner had the strangers left the show grounds, when John Scott, a professional trainer, came to me and asked if I sold my pony. I told him no and asked why he was so interested. He looked at me in amazement and told me about an experience he had a few days before this show.

"About four days ago I got a phone call from a lady in New Jersey. She said she was in the market for a harness show pony." He paused a minute and then, "She told me she had seen the write-ups in the horse magazines about your pony and asked me what I knew about him, and for that matter, about you. Doc, I told her what I knew and said you were supposed to be here at this horse show. Then she asked me if the pony was for sale and I told her I assumed it was. Then she wanted to know how much I wanted for him and I told her I didn't really know, but I knew once you refused three thousand dollars."

I remembered jokingly using that three thousand dollar price while talking to another harness pony owner. Certainly I wasn't serious during that conversation. Then suddenly it dawned on me, and to John Scott too, that this lady had come all of the way from the East Coast to buy the pony realizing that it was going to cost her big money—at least more than the three thousand I reportedly refused! She drove home empty-handed.

Not a bit sorry for what I had done, it went through my mind I wasn't such a good horse trader after all. It also went through my mind that my investment of one hundred and ten green American dollars, less what I recovered when I sold the buggy and the harness, would have netted nearly enough money to start my daughter in college. The Clinic Orderly won many championships and was retired at a tearful ceremony some years later in Huntington, West Virginia.

There is one more story about this marvelous little animal. The same summer I turned down the sale to the lady from New Jersey, we were showing horses at another county fair in Ohio. The grandstand was built right up to the edge of the show ring and if a spectator desired, it was close enough he could reach out and touch the horses as they went by. The harness show pony class was called, and Terri and The Clinic Orderly were the first ones in the show ring. As she made her first pass in front of the crowd, her pony, in tune with the excitement, broke his gait and attempted to run. Terri and Tonto had been well-schooled and I had no fear about her animal causing any trouble. Like a real professional horseman she shook the pony's head with the driving lines to get his absolute attention and at the same time she shouted, "Come up here—damn you!" The crowd heard every word and responded with spontaneous applause along with an outburst of laughter. Mother was embarrassed no end, as was I, but she came by her swearing honestly, as on occasion I had been known to use such words. When the judge handed in his final decision, again The Clinic Orderly was the grand champion. Six-year-old Terri and her pony got a standing ovation.

Terri never wanted her pony sold, and true to her wishes, he never was.

This grand little champion lived many years and when my daughter married, she and her husband had three boys. When her children were little, they too were entertained by him. He now rests peacefully, buried in a hillside grave overlooking our farm. He was a victim of a severe case of colic while I was out of town.

§   §   §

The people of my part of America clung to the horse as a grand creature long after the automobile came into being. I think owning a horse gives a person a feeling of accomplishment and certainly having a winning show ring animal gives the owner a lot of pride and prestige. And then, owning a horse is just part of being a Kentuckian and all of us are proud of that! I have a friend here in my town that sums it up. He says, "The outside of a horse is good for the inside of a man." He might be right.

My horse practice spawned many interesting stories and revealed some unusual people. I treated sick horses, repaired wounds and administered vaccines. As a veterinary surgeon I was called on to castrate, or as the hill people say, "work on," stud horses, bulls, boar hogs and even cats and dogs. Surgical removal of the male animals' testes stop the male sex drive and aggressiveness. The animal was then easier and safer to handle. The neutered stallions became geldings, the bulls were turned into steers and the boars were just plain old hogs after I worked on them. The cats and dogs were referred to as neutered animals.

Most horse owners did not have the facilities or the knowledge to handle a mature stallion so they had them "cut." Some veterinary surgeons gave the horse a light anesthetic and with a casting harness laid him down and tied him up and then operated. Some of us who did a lot of this work developed a technique where we operated on the horse in a standing position. A nose twitch to get the horses attention, a medical tranquilizer to ease his apprehension, and a rope tied in his tail then thrown over a rafter to get the weight off of the horse's rear feet was all that was necessary. The operation was done quickly, no chance of injuring the horse when you laid him down and no anesthetic risk was involved. I preferred the standing procedure and so did my horse owners.

Buddy Kirby was a Tennessee Walking Horse trainer who grew up in the business. His father was a trainer before him and I suppose if there are offspring, they are training horses too. At the time of this incident, Buddy was employed by a group of four medical doctors in Paintsville, Kentucky, a coal mining town, "up Sandy" in the big hill country, to train and manage a large show stable. These doctors were all well-to-do, serving patients from the coal fields in that area. Buddy called me one day and wanted me to come to his barn and castrate a stallion. He also told me his bosses, all MDs, were going to be there to watch me do the operation. This young trainer was my good friend and then he added, "Doc, one of these men told me if they could see you cut a horse one time, they were good enough surgeons they wouldn't need a vet anymore! Then one of 'em even asked me why give some of that coal mine money away if he could do it himself?"

Buddy and I discussed this over the phone and being forewarned, I suggested we just go along with their game but make a few changes to suit ourselves. He laughed at my suggestion and said, "Doggone it, Doc, that'll tear 'em up!"

I drove seventy miles to Paintsville and sure enough, I had an audience. The barn was full of MD spectators! I went through the introductions and the handshakes and the offer of a cold beer or a drink of good whiskey whichever I wanted. Of course I refused. It was obvious these doctors were trying to make a party of this at my expense. I went through a big production about proper sterilization of the instruments and handling my equipment. I didn't want any criticism from these people. I laid out the syringe along with a bottle of tranquilizer. I had previously removed the label because these MDs didn't need to know what I was using. Then I told Buddy to get my patient. He already knew how I did these operations because he had helped me do several in his dad's training barn in another Kentucky town. Before I drove to Paintsville, I coached him how I intended to handle this situation. He and I had the trap set! I had my lariat rope tossed over a rafter in the corner of a box stall. Buddy put the nose twitch on the horse and, turning my back on my audience, I injected the tranquilizer into the horse's jugular vein, at the same time muttering some mumbo-jumbo, just like some doctors do when they are trying to impress a patient. Buddy and I maneuvered the horse into the corner, tied the rope to his tail and told a barn man that was helping us to pull it up tight. The doctors crowded closer. They were eager for what they thought was to be their lesson in veterinary surgery. One of them, addressing his remarks to me like it was an order said, "Hey, Doc, wait 'till I get me a cold beer before you start."

By this time I was fed up with the whole thing and with a motion to Buddy, he tightened the twitch around the horse's upper lip and, before the drinker could pop a cap on his beer bottle, I crowded under the colt and had him castrated. My onlookers never saw a thing because it happened so quick. Of course, out of professional courtesy I got accolades and admiration for my work and expertise. I am certain that every one of those four doctors knew I was aware of their plan and I am sure by now they were a little embarrassed at what they had done. Nothing was ever said again about these human practitioners stepping over the line into my profession. Buddy and I later chuckled and we admired our performance too.

§   §   §

Actually I use the term horse doctor loosley. I like and work with all kinds of equine critters, including mules, burros, ponies and even exotics like zebras. On occasion some of these animals provoked interesting or even bizarre incidents in my daily practice.

About eleven o'clock on a sunny, summer Saturday morning I got a phone call from the chief of the Ashland Fire Department Emergency Squad. He was nearly in a panic and shouted over the telephone, "Doc, we need your help—quick!" He caught his breath, finally lowered his voice and explained that a horse somehow got out of his pasture and when the owner tried to catch him, he bolted, ran down the railroad right-of-way onto a trestle where he fell when his legs slipped through the cross ties. "We have exhausted every effort and we need you now!" He emphasized the word "now." I drove to the scene of the accident and by the time I arrived, there must have been at least one hundred people standing around waiting to see if I could do anything to help this poor horse.

The horse was in a lather of sweat and covered with cuts and scratched places where he had struggled, trying to get up. Every time someone tried to get close to this poor animal, it seemed to panic and struggle more. Sizing up the situation, I filled my syringe with a potent tranquilizer and injected it into my frustrated horse patient. In just a short time he calmed down and stopped struggling. A murmur of appreciation went through my audience!

And then, just like in a melodrama, the unbelievable happened! Here came a train, the engineer blowing the steam whistle for the crossing! This was high drama. Everyone in the crowd scattered except one thoughtful fireman who ran down the track toward the locomotive waving his arms trying to get the engineer to stop the train. With a puff of steam and a swish of air, the engineer pulled on the brakes and stopped the locomotive just before he got to the bridge. He and his helper climbed down from the cab and offered to help us if they could.

All of this time my mind had been searching for a solution and perhaps, I thought, if we could get a sheet of plywood, we could slide it under the horse's front legs. Since a horse gets up with its front feet first, maybe he could get a foothold on the plywood and we could lead him away. I made my suggestion and in short order two men appeared with a four-by-eight sheet of three-quarter-inch plywood. With some manpower, we managed to slide the wood under the horse's chest. With a little more manpower, two of us pulled one leg up out of the space between the cross ties and put the horse's foot on the board. We did the same thing with the other leg. Then without any effort at all, just as if the horse knew what we planned, he got up and let himself be led away. I treated the cuts and bruises, accepted the thanks from the onlookers and then found out the man who was to pay my bill had led his horse over the hill and was gone! One of the firemen volunteered to pay me but I refused and chalked it off as my good deed for the day. I guess I figured my reward as hero-of-the-day was enough. The next morning the owner did show up at my office and paid his bill in full with cash.

§   §   §

Animal behavior is a complex subject. It is perplexing at times to the owner who then comes to the veterinarian for answers. Sometimes these answers are hard to find. Other times the solutions just happen and are often used to an advantage. Observation by a smart animal trainer of these happenings is a useful tool, and these traits are often developed into part of the animal's routine. In a remote sort of a way, this unusual behavior fit one of my professional adventures.

On the Fourth of July, shortly after the experience with the horse on the railroad trestle, the American Legion Post in Russell, a railroad community just west of Ashland, sold chances on a Mexican Burro. The organization advertised this animal would make a nice child's pet, be an asset to any stable and keep dogs out of the sheep pastures! Bold statements and a good sales pitch. A former Russell resident who now lived in New Mexico had donated the burro for the occasion. The ad read the little donkey would be shipped by train and would arrive on the Fourth of July in time for the ticket drawing. With this notice was a small P.S.—"This animal has been captured on public range land and will probably need some training."

The man in charge of this raffle was Ray Campbell. Ray was a nervous little fellow, full of enthusiasm for everything he did, a pillar in the community's affairs and a true lover of horse flesh. He was certainly the right man for this burro project. His vocation was driving a steam locomotive on the railroad, and his eyes bulged and his chest swelled with pride when he talked about pulling the lanyard that blew the engine's steam whistle as he approached a crossing. He also puffed up with pride when he talked about his avocation, which was showing his ponies at the local horse shows. Mrs. Campbell, and I am sure other relatives and lesser associates, called him by his given name—Ray. Everybody else called him "Little Buddy." I did too and even his records in my clinic files list him as "Little Buddy Campbell."

Little Buddy contacted me and asked if I would be on hand when the burro arrived. I assured him I would and volunteered what I could to make the celebration a success. I was among the crowd when the train arrived and the railroad car was spotted on a siding alongside of a loading dock. Four men rushed to the freight car, opened the door and there, confined in a big wooden crate, was a frightened little donkey, his eyes blinking at the sudden flood of bright outside light. Both of his ears were sticking out of the top of the crate. I am sure if burros think, this one was wondering what was going to happen to him next! Eventually the four men got the crate out of the boxcar onto the dock. The crowd roared its approval. Reaching through the slats of the crate, Campbell and one of his helpers fastened two heavy ropes to the burro's halter. Finally it was announced to the onlookers that the burro would be temporarily taken to Mr. Campbell's barn for a brief rest, a drink of water and some feed. The drawing for a winner's name was scheduled for later in the day.

In the meantime I was standing by the crate, stethoscope hung around my neck, getting ready to examine the animal as the committee had suggested. As I stood there watching, a reporter from the local newspaper asked if I would mind if they took pictures. Of course I agreed, savoring all of the free publicity I could get for me and my clinic. With my stethoscope I went through the motions of listening for heart and lung sounds. I did all of this through the slats of the crate that held the star of the show, our frightened little gray burro.

A wrecking bar made quick work of the crate and all seemed to go well. The newspaper photographer asked me if I would do the examination one more time so he could get more photographs. With a lot of apprehension, I again went through my stethoscope routine. Flash bulbs flashed and for a moment all went well, then I stepped back out of harm's way because I knew, sooner or later, something was bound to happen. Now most people imagine all burros are cute little creatures with long floppy ears and soulful sad eyes. This animal by this time had done some thinking and had it all figured out. Now, instead of the prototype we expected, he had both ears pinned back to his head and the fire of the Devil in his travel-weary, red-rimmed little eyes. Suddenly the donkey made a big lunge and jerked Little Buddy Campbell off his feet and dragged him and his helper ten or twenty feet before help arrived and he was finally stopped!

Little Buddy's house and barn were at the top of a long, steep hill about two blocks from the railroad siding. Now came another challenge. I wondered how in the world they were going to get this untamed animal up the hill to Campbell's barn.

As the crowd watched and wondered what was coming next, a young fellow, shirtless on the hot day, his hair tied down with a bright red bandanna, drove up on his Harley Davidson motorcycle. As he braked to a stop, in true biker's fashion, he revved up the engine—I guess to announce his arrival. This kind of noise obviously was never heard in the desert of New Mexico and the startled burro, in his fright and by absolute chance, charged up the hill toward Little Buddy's house! After about one hundred yards, though, he stopped and no tugging or pulling by the two men holding the ropes could get him to move. I followed the two men and their charge and by now was close to the Harley driver. As a joke I said, "Do it again. Maybe we can get him all the way up the hill." Taking me at my word, the rider twisted the throttle on his bike and the engine roared. The donkey bucked and jumped and hit the ground, running straight up the hill toward a drink and something to eat. The crowd, impressed by the unexpected activity, roared its approval for the bike-rider as he herded the donkey and its handlers up the hill toward the barn lot. After another brief struggle, the burro was put in the barn. Believe it or not, he calmed down and was never any trouble again. A man from Ohio had the winning ticket and I heard later that the burro lived a long, peaceful life. This episode doesn't have a thing to do with veterinary medicine but as a student of animal behavior, I am glad I was there to see the motorcycle routine.

§   §   §

No days were ever the same; each brought its own surprises. Not a week after the burro incident I had a phone call from a client in Deering, Ohio, close to the farm where I treated the calves made sick by the rats. This man almost shouted over the phone, "Come quick, Doctor, my horse just got hit by a car and something is stuck in his side!" I told him I would be right there.

I drove as fast as I safely could and in less than a half an hour I was at the scene of the accident. The driver of the car, a Pontiac, had lost control of his vehicle, bounced across the drainage ditch through a wire fence into the pasture and hit the horse which was minding its own business grazing on the sweet, tender summer grass. When I got there, several people were gathered at the accident site at the side of the road. The car, with its front end smashed, was still halfway through the fence. Two men were holding the injured horse which was sweating and appeared to be in a state of shock. Sure enough, just like the owner told me over the phone, there was a large piece of metal protruding from the animal's side.

This metal object was the hood ornament off of the car. It was an Indian Chief replica, headdress and all, and was the signature of the Pontiac automobile. The trailing headdress acted like an arrow barb and prevented the metal piece from falling out. I did what I could to ease the animal's pain and after a tricky bit of equine surgery, removed the metal from the wound. I closed the wound with some sutures, administered an anti-tetanus shot and dispensed some medicine to prevent infection. I visited with the owner and we discussed the case. I told him I would be back the next day. This had certainly been a bizarre case. I drove back across the bridge to Kentucky and my office.

It wasn't an hour later when I got another phone call. This one was from John Hord, a client over in Grayson, Kentucky. He too almost shouted over the phone, "Doc, come quick, my ridin' horse just got hit by a car and he's got somethin' stuck in his side!" I couldn't believe what I just heard. It was like a record playing the same tune again.

I drove the twenty miles to John's farm and, sure enough, here was a horse, hit by a car, an almost identical case to the one I had just come from in Ohio! A hood ornament from the same model Pontiac was sticking out of the horse's side—only instead of being on the left side, this poor horse got it from the right! I felt by this time like I was an expert, and after doing my barnyard surgery and telling John Hord about the injured horse in Ohio, I drove back to Ashland. I practiced thirty-nine years in Kentucky and never saw a case like either of these again. I doubt very many veterinarians ever saw one Pontiac hood ornament injury, much less two in one day!

§   §   §

The horse practice was going well, but so was the small animal practice. My new clinic facility drew many new clients, even though I did mostly large animal work and I constantly suppressed the tales that "Doc Martin is strictly a large animal vet. Take your dogs and cats someplace else." This stigma held for years and, later, after I gave up all of the large animal work, I still heard that story.

June Horton, one of the owners at the stockyard, called and jokingly asked me if I still worked on horse and cows. Of course he knew I did and I inquired what he needed. It didn't take long to find out.

"Doc, come out here to my house quick, my bull got out and gored my good saddle horse." I promised I would be there as soon as I spayed a cat which my helper, Stormy Lemaster, already had on the operating table. Horton's quick reply was, "Hell, Doc, the horse will bleed to death by that time. Can't you come right now?"

June told me blood was pouring from a bad wound in the horse's neck. I immediately assumed it was from the jugular vein and told him to get some big clean towels and press them as hard as he could against the wound to try and stop the hemorrhage. I hung up the phone, told Stormy to put the cat back in its cage and drove as fast as I could to June Horton's farm, about ten miles from the office.

I drove into the yard and sure enough, covered with blood was a ghost-white June Horton, a bloody towel in each hand, trying his best to stop the profuse bleeding from the wound in the horse's neck. I reached into my surgery kit, grabbed a long-nosed hemostat and told June and another fellow who was helping, to try and hold the horse still while I tried to stop the blood. I probed into the wound and with a lucky jab clamped off one side of the laceration. Another hemostat on the other side of the hole stopped the blood from the bleeding vein. I had won round one of the battle. Now I had some time, even though the horse was pale and very unsteady on his feet from the blood loss. I managed to clean up the entire area, irrigate the wound with saline solution and with my needle holder and a large curved suture needle loaded with catgut, managed to ligate the cut vein above and below the jagged tear. Fortunately the horse has a main jugular and also, unlike other animals, it has a another vein we call the recurrent jugular. Both share the job of blood transport, making complete ligation of one or the other possible.

It was a very hot day and, after we were done with the horse, Mrs. Horton insisted her husband and I come in and wash up. At the same time she said she had some cold lemonade in the pitcher. The cleanup and the lemonade both went well. June walked out to the car with me, thanked me profusely for what I had done, paid me in cash and with a big grin on his face, his last remark was, "Go back to your office and spay that damned cat."

§   §   §

Little Buddy Campbell, the burro man, owned two ponies and showed them in road pony classes. Road ponies were the miniature versions of the road horse, which were very much like the old-fashioned buggy horse which could travel pretty fast. There were classes in most horse shows for the road horse as well as the road pony, both exciting and a great spectator event at every show. Little Buddy's best pony was a good one, but he was a stallion and was a problem when there were mares around. On more than one occasion Campbell and I discussed castrating him, but each time I attempted to set up an appointment for the surgery, Little Buddy would find an excuse to put it off. On a September night at the Greenup County Fair Horse Show, this little stallion's libido got the best of him and he became unruly. His was changed from a brilliant star in the show ring to a sex-starved, vicious stud. The horse show judge disqualified Campbell and his pony and told him to have his pony gelded. His pony had hurt another pony and feeling guilt, Campbell made his decision. Little Buddy called me, and I gave him an appointment for the next morning at ten o'clock.

I had no sooner walked in the door at seven-thirty the next day when the phone rang. For some reason, I just knew the caller was Mr. Campbell with an excuse to cancel out! Sure enough, I was right. I asked him why after the show judge had given him an ultimatum to "geld him, or don't come back to this horse show."

"Doc Martin, I was talkin' to Charley Carter and he done told me the sign ain't right to cut a horse." Charley was a local horse trader and like a lot of Kentucky hill people, believed the Zodiac signs were life-commanding and should be followed to the letter! Believe it or not, a lot of my work hinged on the signs being in the right position. Little Buddy paused in his conversation and then asked, "Doc, do you believe in the sign?"

I hesitated just an instant giving Campbell time to listen good and said, "Little Buddy, I don't, but if you really do, it'll turn out better if we do it your way. We can always reschedule the operation." I failed to add as far as I was concerned, when the knife was sharp, the sign was right.

Dead silence then, apparently digesting my thoughts on the sign, he said, "Doc Martin, I don't think I do either. I'll be at your place at ten o'clock." I wasn't sure he would show up.

Stormy and I started on our hospital cases. We spayed a dog and fixed a broken leg on a cat. While I was still in the operating room, the front door buzzer sounded and Stormy left to see who it was. In just a short time my assistant came back and told me Ray Campbell had his pony outside and he had an appointment to have him "fixed." Stormy said, "Doc, he's really in bad shape—crying and jabbering and huggin' on that pony like it was his child." I assured Stormy the pony was like Ray Campbell's child and my assistant said he guessed he understood.

Everything was ready and after reaffirming I thought there was no real truth in the signs, we got the pony out of the horse trailer. I put the casting harness on him, gave him a tranquilizer injection and lay him down on the grass. I usually laid ponies down, since they were too small to get under and do a standing castration. The minute the pony was on his side and I was tying his feet so in his struggle to get up he wouldn't hurt anybody, Campbell was running up and down in the clinic yard, tears streaming down his face, pleading with me—his mind now completely changed—"Please don't cut my pony. Doc, don't hurt him" He even got down on his knees and again said, "Doc, don't hurt him."

In an instant, I made the decision and did my work before Little Buddy, who put his hands over his eyes to block the view, realized it was over. He was dazed. He was still on his knees and he looked up questionably at me about his animal's welfare. I assured him everything was all right and in a few minutes, I untied the ropes and the pony got up on his feet and started picking at the green grass in my yard.

A big, satisfied grin spread all over his face when he saw that the pony, for all practical purposes, was all right. Then I knew I had made the correct decision and if I hadn't made that decision and operated, he would never have had the nerve to come back and reschedule. Campbell wiped the tears from his eyes with his blue railroader's bandanna and he thanked me. We loaded the pony into his trailer and he took him home.

Stormy and I laughed at all of this, but laughed with respect for our friend, and for that matter his pony too. Later in the day, after he hauled his pony home, he came back to the clinic with an apology to me for acting as he did. He brought us a box of candy and paid his bill.

That pony and little Buddy Campbell went on showing for years and I had a friend forever.

§   §   §

Not every day was full of fun and excitement in my horse practice. Some days nothing went right. I had it figured out when everything got well and lived, you were the greatest doctor in the world; when they died, you got the blame! Tommy Franklin was one of the neighborhood horsemen. He owned a beautiful palomino stallion, which he showed at the smaller shows in trail horse classes. He also spent many happy hours on trail rides with his other horse owner friends.

After a long spell of cold, wet weather the sun finally graced the earth, and they planned a trail ride of twenty miles. One of the riders mentioned it to me and I remarked that after a long layup, they should be sure not to overdo it and expose the horse to azoturia. This was the proper name for a disease the old-time dray drivers who hauled beer and freight, used to call "Monday morning sickness." This condition invariably happened when the horse went back to work after a weekend rest, still on full feed. The disease was easy to diagnose and if not too severe, was easy to treat with professional help. Those that went untreated, and some of the more severe cases, died.

Monday evening I was in the clinic barn medicating a horse recovering from a throat operation. This case was doing well and the horse was ready to be sent home. I heard somebody in back of the barn shout, "Doc Martin, for God's sake come quick!" I looked away from my sore throat patient and there was Tommy Franklin in a state of absolute hyper-excitement. I stepped out of the stall and he grabbed my arm and steered me behind my barn to the street, where I saw his pretty golden palomino horse crumpled on the ground obviously in death's throes. I questioned him about the horse and he told me they had ridden a long distance with no trouble until the last thirty minutes. The horse seemed a little stiff but after moving about, appeared to get better. Everything seemed OK until he got about a mile from my clinic and then he stiffened up and refused to move. It took him all kinds of urging to get him the rest of the way. I rushed up the hill to my office and got some medicine and ran back down the hill and tried to save the horse's life. He died, in spite of what I tried to do, in a matter of minutes.

All I heard for the next week from the horse people was, "Doc Martin killed Tommy Franklin's horse."

These unusual cases didn't happen every day, but when they did they added flavor—tasty or not—to our everyday life. It was obvious the bad and the heartbreak had to come with the good rewards.

§   §   §

One cold, rainy fall day I spent the entire day blood-testing a big herd of beef cattle. It was after dark when I got home, dead tired, chilled to the bone from the cold rain and ready to go to bed. Then the telephone rang, reminding me my day might not yet be over. I hoped I wouldn't have to go out again.

The caller was Vernon Rice. He lived thirty miles away over in West Virginia. Vernon was a horse trainer, but he really served two jobs. It was hard to tell which one he liked best. His daytime job was driving a beer delivery truck and his self-established bonus on that job was all the free beer he could drink! On his days off and at night his other passion was training Tennessee Walking Horses. He did that job very well and drank a lot of beer on that job too! At the time, Vernon was working for Dr. Glover, a physician who practiced up in the mountains of West Virginia. The doctor owned several nice Tennessee Walkers, but his pride and joy was a stallion named Midnight Gold Sun. This fancy horse had just recently been crowned a champion at the world famous Tennessee Walking Horse Celebration—the ultimate show for walking horse owners.

Excitement charged the phone lines that night as Vernon told me he thought Gold Sun had something caught in his throat. In a panic he shouted into the phone, "Hurry up Doc, I think this old stud horse is choked. For God's sake come right away!" It took me over an hour of driving through the cold and the rain to get to Vernon's barn.

Sure enough, the horse exhibited every evidence of being choked. He stood with his head extended and at times, trying to get the foreign body loose, shook his head, ropes of saliva flying from his mouth. With Vernon's help I passed a stomach tube and forced the blocked object down into the horse's stomach. Vernon seeing the choke was gone, blurted, "Thank God, Doc, you done it!" Gold Sun wasn't so explosive but he did turn his head and looked at me with what seemed to be a word of thanks. He was relieved and frankly, so was I.

The situation resolved, we went into the tack room where it was warm and I went to the sink to wash my hands and the stomach tube.

I took off my coveralls, washed and disinfected my rubber boots and got my equipment ready to put back in my car. While I was doing this I asked Vernon if he had any idea what had choked his horse. Before answering, he stepped over to the corner of the room, reached into a cooler and got us both a can of beer. Looking me straight in the eye he said in a quiet, but positive tone of voice, "A damned rat!"

I hardly knew what to think at this remark. I was amazed. I gasped, "What are you talking about?" I opened the beer can, took a long swallow and said, "What do you mean a rat?"

"Doc, this barn's full of mice and rats. They come here in the hay. Well this old stud will bite at anything that moves in his stall and earlier tonight I saw a great big rat run along the tail board and I saw old Gold Sun make a lunge for it. He missed that one but I'm almost certain he grabbed at another one and somehow must have gulped and the rat got stuck in his throat!"

An amazing story. Now, while the horse was digesting the rat, we both toasted the stallion and finished our beer. Midnight Gold Sun made an uneventful recovery and went on to win many Walking Horse championships. Vernon Rice continued working at both of his jobs and—drinking his beer.

§   §   §

The horse industry, and for that matter the entire practice, too, spawned many interesting and sometimes humorous stories, but don't get the idea that all of my work was fun-and-animal games. Most of it was still hard physical labor, but the rewards for participating were worth the efforts. Part of the practice of veterinary medicine involves public health programs and the prevention of diseases related to animals and man, examples being the Bang's disease and tuberculosis programs.

One day in the early sixties, a small article in our newspaper told about a new horse disease just discovered in south Texas. The story was not too exciting to most readers but it immediately caught my attention. The newspaper release called the outbreak Venezuelan Equine Encephalitis. It was a big name for a disease I had never heard of. The newspaper shortened it to VEE.

In a matter of weeks, VEE was spreading northward and had infected many horses along the Rio Grande River. Rumor had it the disease had been deliberately introduced by a Third World enemy country into Mexico hoping it would spread north into the United States. Rumor also suggested this was an experimental move by the enemy, whoever that was, for possible introduction of a disease that would infect people. There was no question VEE had some serious implications, threatening not only the entire horse industry, but perhaps human health as well.

The Department of Animal Industry set the stage to try and stop VEE from spreading. The plan was to vaccinate every equine—mules, horses, donkeys or what have you—against the disease. The mass immunization program was to extend from Texas and its adjoining states north to the Ohio River. It was a tremendous undertaking and the last state to the north to be involved was Kentucky. Once again the large animal veterinarians responded to a government control program.

The Kentucky Department of Agriculture established the guidelines for the project in our state with the University of Kentucky's County Agricultural Extension Agents arranging the clinic locations—usually four different places every day. The state supplied fresh vaccine every morning to a distribution point from which it was in turn delivered to each participating veterinarian. Our supply point was West Liberty, a small country town thirty five miles away. The veterinarian's wife there made her rounds early every morning delivering the day's anticipated doses.

My first clinic was held at my office. Everybody in the vicinity of Ashland brought their animals. It was like a huge parade as they lined up for several city blocks! I had no idea there were that many horses, ponies and mules almost in my own back yard. The owner held his animal, I injected the vaccine, my wife filled in vaccination certificates and one of my clinic helpers fastened a metal tag into the hair of the horse's tail. The vaccinations were free to the owner; the state paid the veterinarian a small fee per head for his services. When we were done at my clinic, we moved to a predetermined rural location for the next clinic. Again, I was amazed at how many equines still were kept in our modern day of paved roads and automobiles.

At first we saw just riding horses and ponies. As we worked our way back into the hill country with our clinics, we started seeing some really good draft horses and mules. Now, I really like a mule. There is something about that long-eared animal that makes a lot of sense. First of all, he is smarter than a horse. Examples: when a horse gets tired he never stops. When a mule gets tired he says it's time to take a break and rest! A hot, overworked horse will gorge itself on water and suffer the consequences of colic, founder or other nasty ailments. A mule stops when he drinks enough to satisfy his immediate thirst. A good mule is worth a lot of money. In my county, Claude Groves, my sawmill friend, always had a mule or two. Lace Hardin still owned Barney and Sam, the two good critters that pulled me out of the winter snow and mud some winters past. Bill Crider at the Highland Dairy Farm owned a pair of mules with the longest ears I ever saw! Crider's mules were there for Bill Crider's personal pleasure. He was like me—he loved a mule. And, there were others scattered through the county on isolated hill farms where a man and tractor never dared to go.

As we worked our way deeper into the big hill country we saw more and more mules, all tended to by proud owners. There were matched teams of sorrels, bays and even white mules, all in prime condition. We saw many saddle mules whose owners swore were better than any horse they ever straddled. These animals came from far and wide, some driven in a buggy, some ridden, some hand-walked over long distances to get the free protection. One nice lady from out in the Blaine Creek area told me she had ridden her mule twelve miles to get to this clinic and as she was telling me this, she was affectionately wiping the sweat from her mule's face with her own handkerchief!

While the main reason for the clinics was to immunize the equines, the clinics also were a socializing place, especially in the hill country. At a clinic in Lawrence County, the next county south of Ashland, it was sorghum molasses-making time. Besides the crowds of horses, ponies and mules there for their "shots," there were crowds of people helping make the "lasses." Some were hauling the sorghum cane to the press, others were busy stirring the cooking vats and a few kept a plentiful supply of fire wood on hand. The focal point of the festivity was a lone mule harnessed to the pole of the sorghum press, walking slowly around the circle, squeezing the juices from the cane. Sitting on the ground beside the press, a local preacher, a master sorghum-maker, fed the cane into the crude machine. At my suggestion, he stopped the mule for just a moment and I gave it the vaccine. The preacher stuffed more cane into the mill and after a click of his tongue and a "git up, mule," the animal started his trips around the circle again. After all of the animals were vaccinated, we stayed for a while sampling the fresh-made sorghum by dipping a cane stalk into the vats of boiling cane juice and licking it off like a lollipop!

Before we finished this program I saw some wonderful saddle horses and ponies that were home-grown and hand-raised on the hill country farms. These animals, with a little dressing up, were every bit as good as the high-priced horses we took to the horse shows. Draft horses were common too and were proudly presented to me for my praise and attention by their owners. And at one location I vaccinated ten mine ponies and a small mule the owner called a "bank mule." Bank mules were used in the mines too and even though they never worked deep in the mines like the ponies, according to this owner, ". . . this son-of a bitch is worth his weight in gold." He said it with sincere affection!

I have no idea how many animals I vaccinated but it was well over a thousand before the clinics were finished.

This program went on most of the early summer and before it was over, every horse, donkey, pony and mule in the Commonwealth of Kentucky was immunized against this disease. Unlike the compulsory Bang's and TB testing programs there was no dissention; the owners wanted all of the protection they could get for their animals. It was a huge undertaking, involving thousands of animals and most of the southern and southwestern states, but it was successful. We, "in the line of duty," beat whoever sent this virus north to hurt us!

§   §   §

These are but a few of the horse-mule-pony situations I found myself in over those early years. The results were very rewarding and I am proud, in spite of the not-so-kind remarks by some, that I was known and respected as a good horse doctor.

The Tobacco Patch Airstrip

B<small>Y THE TIME THE SIXTIES GOT HERE, THE</small> M<small>OHRLAND</small> S<small>TABLES WAS OUT OF</small> business and my growing stable of show horses was housed in the clinic barn. When my wife and I finished building Jomar, we moved our stock into the new saddle-horse barn at the farm. This gave us space in the clinic barn which soon was filled with hospital cases. This move also divided my attention from the clinic to the farm and training the horses.

Be it understood, I was really a horse enthusiast, not a horse trainer, and I realized a professional trainer would be an asset to me and my stable.

On a hot August night at a horse show in southern Ohio, Chuck Shultz came to my stalls and asked me to come look at a cut on a horse's leg. Chuck was currently the trainer-manager of Murray Heights Farm, a large saddle horse establishment in the heart of the Blue Grass in Lexington, Kentucky. Most people considered him one of the best trainers in the business. I examined and treated his injured horse, and after I was done he and I had a long conversation about horses and especially about veterinarians. Then he asked me if I would do all of his work. I was flattered and agreed to accept the job even though it added one hundred and ten miles, each way, to my already over-stretched practice territory. Chuck, and his wife Helen, were both from my hometown, and it was maybe this, as well as my professsional reputation, that started this association. It was a wedding of convenience for both of us. Shultz had his horse doctor; I had my horse trainer.

Murray Heights Farm was a beautiful farm with old, stately buildings, a big modern horse barn and rolling acres of cultured Blue Grass pastures all fenced with traditional wooden fences, the trademark of the Kentucky horse farms. Chuck and Helen lived in the big old farmhouse at the main entrance only fifty yards from the saddle horse barn.

My work for Chuck was routine. I would drive the one hundred ten miles to the farm each week and go through the entire barn worming horses, dressing teeth, treating any ailing animal or discussing management problems that my expertise could solve. On occasion Chuck would have a sick horse, and if we couldn't solve the problem by telephone, I would make the long drive and look at that animal. It wasn't long before Bob Davis, owner of Wing May Farm at Paris, Kentucky, wanted me to do his work too. This offer was flattering. These farms were two of the very best American Saddle Horse farms in an area saturated with veterinarians, all widely known as expert equine practitioners. I agreed to do Davis's work too, if I could do it the same day I was attending Chuck Shultz's horses. This worked for a while, but I soon found out the time on the road was too much and it interfered with my already established clinic practice.

On one of the trips to Chuck's stable, I met Mr. Loyd Rouse, a man from Michigan who had some horses in training with Chuck. He owned an airplane and flew to Lexington every week to see his horses. By chance Mary Helen and I were there one weekend and met this man and his daughter. During the course of our conversation, our new acquaintance asked about our farm and horses, knowing I was an airplane pilot in World War II, the conversation got around to aviation. The first thing he asked me was why I didn't fly anymore. I explained how after the war I was a flight instructor at the airport in my town in Ohio and even continued as an instructor when I went to college at Ohio State University. Available time and the lack of money soon grounded me, and I directed all my attention toward my college work. As a matter of fact, I explained I had gone out of my way to avoid airports, trying to put the temptation of flying out of my mind! He looked at me and said, "I don't understand—why?" I never answered that question. Then he asked me about the closest airport to our farm and indicated he and his daughter would someday like to come visit us.

"Tri-State Airport in Huntington, West Virginia, is twelve miles from our house. If you ever do decide to come, call me and I will meet you at the airport." Mary Helen and I drove back home, never giving any more thought to Rouse, his daughter or his flying machine.

Two weeks later he called. I drove to Huntington and picked him up. It was a beautiful Sunday morning and we had a nice visit at Jomar discussing our horses and the farm. After our visit I drove them back to the airport, and then it happened. My Michigan friend said, "Doctor, I am in no hurry, let me take you a ride in my airplane."

Never hesitating I said, "I am ready."

He let me fly his airplane. It was a nice Cessna, all decked out with fancy gadgets and mind-boggling instruments. The basic airplane was the same, but the equipment and the gadgets had certainly changed since my days in China and Burma! I managed the takeoff and flew out over Jomar and eventually returned to the airport. I suggested he land the airplane, since my veterinary expertise was far better than my flying ability at that time.

When I got back home I told Mary Helen what had happened. She said, "You are hooked now!" And for sure I was. The very next week I had a flight physical, went to the Ashland airport and took two flying lessons. It was like riding a bicycle, once you learned, it soon comes back to you.

Time, hard work and good fortune had improved my financial status and with this improvement, and Loyd Rouse's timely association, I had the urge to fly again. Not only had I missed the excitement and fun of aviation, but now the practice covered such a large area, I thought it could be a handy transportation tool. I didn't have to linger too long thinking about it.

That same week I bought my first airplane. It was shining bright red Piper Tri-Pacer. Being an old aviator, I was impressed with the radios and navigation instruments which were far superior to those we had in our old military aircraft. Being a horseman, I was impressed with the power of its tiny engine. Underneath the cowling was the power of one hundred sixty Clydesdales! My new airplane had a high wing, was short coupled and very fast. It was like a sports car of the air and was fun to fly.

I polished and shined and practiced flying my new airplane and it wasn't very long until I was once again a proficient pilot. I flew every opportunity I had and the more adept I became, the more I realized that aviation was going to play a part of my life. This happened in the spring of 1966.

I called Shultz and told him about buying the airplane, asking if it would be too much trouble for him to meet me at the Lexington airport on my next scheduled visit even though the airport was fifteen or more miles from Murray Heights Farm. On my next visit, just as we planned, Chuck met me and I did my day's work for him. While I was there, Bob Davis at Wing May Farm called and said he needed me. I told him to come pick me up and we would go to his farm.

The drive from Lexington to Paris took us on quaint, narrow, country roads lined on each side with beautiful Kentucky farms. Most were fenced in either black or white board fences, while a few still had field stone walls built by the slaves in pre-Civil War days. Brood mares and colts grazed in the pastures and an occasional herd of pure-bred cattle added variety to the scene. This was horse heaven—absolutely—and secretly I reveled in my being part of it. I finished my work there and Davis volunteered to drive me to the airport.

I was back at home in less than an hour! Total travel time by air was less than half of the driving time in one direction! This arrangement worked very well. Later, I acquired another farm close to Paris. It was good business.

On a later trip to the Blue Grass, I finished my work early and Chuck suggested that since it was such a pretty day, we get the tractor, drive it out to one of his stock ponds and collect a mess of bullfrogs. First he stopped by his office and picked up a twenty-two caliber rifle and a box of shells. He put the bullets in his pocket, handed me the gun and, at his suggestion, I climbed onto the drawbar of the tractor. We drove across the field to a big pond. Chuck drove slowly around the edge of the water and we saw lots of big frogs. They were at the water's edge, oblivious to the noise of the tractor, soaking up the summer sunshine. They never moved as we drove along the bank. Finally Chuck stopped the tractor, I handed him the rifle and in a few minutes he shot enough frogs to fill a big water bucket! On the way back to the house he promised to put the dressed frog legs in the freezer, and we would have a good meal the next time Mary Helen and I were both there.

Before we got back to the barn, I suggested we drive over to an old to-bacco bed and let me see if it was long enough for a landing strip. With long strides I stepped off and mentally measured the level area to make sure I could take off and land my airplane. It was long enough but there were power lines at one end of my tobacco patch airstrip that might present prob-lems when it came to take off and climb out. I pondered about this and after some calculation, and remembering some of the tricks we used flying out of muddy, war-torn airstrips in China and Burma, I made up my mind I could do it. The idea suited Chuck, since it meant he didn't have the long drive across town to the big airport. When I got back to Ashland, I called Bob Davis and told him about my plan. This would, if everything went OK, work very well. I had visions of flying to Lexington, working at all three of the farms and being back home in less time than it takes to drive it both ways by car. This was the advantage to the flying business.

On the next planned trip I loaded my veterinary supplies in the back seat of my Tri-Pacer and took off for Lexington. There wasn't a cloud in the sky and it looked like you could see for a hundred miles. Turning west I looked over the hills of northern Kentucky. They were soothing with their soft tones of green. To my right I followed the Ohio River for some miles as it wandered down the big valley to the west. Finally the hill country stopped abruptly and the level land of the Blue Grass area was just ahead sprinkled with fine farms and crisscrossed by big highways. Appalachia was behind me; this was different kind of Kentucky. The clear day opened up the entire scenerio—it was truly an aviator's day! Forty-five minutes later I spotted the Murray farm and circled for my landing. I turned in on final approach, lowered full landing flaps and made a perfect landing with plenty of room to spare. I thought to myself "this is a piece of cake!" I taxied right up to the barn where Chuck and Helen were waiting for me. But, before I got out of my airplane, I took a hard look at the power lines I had to get over at the end of the field. From that angle they looked taller and more awesome than ever!

We went to the barn and I wormed six horses and dressed the teeth on two young horses. We discussed some proposed work for the future and after an hour or so, I was done. The other two farms had nothing for me to do on this trip.

I cleaned up my equipment and Chuck and I walked from the barn to the airplane. He helped me load my gear and I said my goodbyes and started thinking about my flight back home. The first thing was to get the airplane airborne and over the power lines at the end of the homemade airstrip. I started the engine, managed a weak wave goodbye to Chuck and Helen and taxied very slowly back to the end of the tobacco patch. Turning into the direction of take off, I checked my engine instruments, ran the power up for a magneto check and dropped a notch of wing flaps for added lift. Everything was in order; then I held the brakes and added full power. With the airplane vibrating under the strain of the full engine power, I released the brakes and the airplane lurched forward and with the added lift from the flaps, it leaped into the air like a frightened bird! I cleared the wires with plenty of room. I leveled off and rocked my wings as a farewell salute to my friends and headed east back toward Ashland. Then I relaxed and suddenly realized I was drenched in the cold sweat of anxiety! I couldn't remember ever going through this before even during my days as a war-time pilot.

I made many trips to the Lexington area and used the tobacco patch landing field many times. Then one day Shultz called me and told me I would have to start going to the big airport in town. It was time to set out the tobacco crop.

I had other horse clients in far away areas that were served by me and the little red flying machine. Fred Culp in Gallipolis, Ohio, had parade horses. I made at least two trips to service his animals. Emmett Ebenhack at Circleville, Ohio, had a barn full of standard-bred racing horses. Circleville was over one hundred miles from home and many hours driving was done away with by using the airplane. Other calls were made to Pikeville, Kentucky, and up in the mountain country of West Virginia. I made trips to Nashville to work for Ringling Brothers, Barnum & Bailey Circus and to Frankfort, Kentucky, to professional meetings. The airplane was a time saver and a money maker. It was also my other passion—flying.

THE CIRCUS

THE YEAR BEFORE I GRADUATED FROM VETERINARY COLLEGE, ANOTHER ONE of the seeds was planted. This came about in a strange way, and I am sure if Granny Riffe, the mountain lady with the sow that couldn't have her pigs, were around today, she would probably say, "Doc Martin, it's got to be part of God's Plan."

One morning while drinking my breakfast coffee and just before going to school, Mary Helen looked at me and said, "Honey, do you like a circus?"

"Sure I do, everybody likes the circus." To the best of my knowledge this was the first time during our marriage the circus had ever been mentioned.

"That's great! I'll make you a deal." Before I could say anything, she said, "I know you like the county fairs and the horse shows and I will go with you to them if you take me to the circuses when they come around."

"What made you ask me such a question?" I was really surprised at what prompted this conversation.

Without waiting for me to utter another word, she said, "I have a girl friend who is a circus star." Then she told me about her friend.

"One summer, when I was a little girl, the Cole Brothers' Circus came to Portsmouth and the circus train was parked on a railroad siding just a block away from our house. It was on the other side of the Tracy Park on Tenth Street. Uncle Henri and I stood on our porch and watched the excitement and commotion as the show folks went about their business unloading the tents, wagons and animals from the train. Animals were everywhere—there were lots of horses and ponies and some zebras and donkeys too."

I could see the excitement mounting in my wife's eyes just like she was seeing it all over again! Then she went on with her story.

"We watched a big herd of elephants and some camels being lined up

173

while their handlers talked to them, keeping them under control." There was excitement in her voice as she went on, "Under the shade of one of those big oak trees a man was holding two llamas. Horses and ponies were tied to the side of the railroad cars while their grooms and keepers waited for the signal to start the parade to the circus lot. Another group of workers unloaded a string of canvas-covered wagons and from the roars and growls that came from these hidden dens, it was obvious these were the cages that housed the lions and tigers." Mary Helen paused as if she was trying to remember more and at the same time let the picture of these happenings settle in my mind. Then she continued her story. "While Uncle Henri and I were watching all of this, a man and a young girl about my age got off of the train and walked down the street away from the crowd. They stopped in front of my house when they saw us standing on the porch.

The man addressing himself to Uncle Henri, said, "Sir, we are looking for a dry goods store. I want to buy some yarn. Can you tell us where to go?"

"I was absolutely spellbound by these people, and my uncle and I walked with them the few blocks downtown and took them to Marting's department store."

My wife went on to tell me that the afternoon with these two was the beginning of a lifelong friendship between her and the little girl. The man was Ernest Clarke. He was the greatest flying trapeze artist of his time and perhaps even of all times! He had the reputation of being the first to routinely complete the triple somersault from the flying trapeze. The young lady with him was his daughter, Ernestine. She followed in the family tradition and made her own reputation as a bareback rider and a trapeze artist. "Ernestine, or Ernie as her daddy called her, and I developed a friendship which has lasted a long time and we still keep in touch with each other. Now I'd like to visit the circus again."

I made my promise as she suggested and went on to my class.

It was a long way from our house to the university and I usually rode the streetcar to school. As the trolley clattered up High Street, I was still thinking about this conversation, and my wandering mind brought back vivid memories of an experience I had at a circus when I was about six years old.

My grandparents lived in Ashland, Kentucky, and on a visit there one summer, grandpa and grandmother and Uncle Fred took me to see the Hagenbeck-Wallace Circus. It was hot and dusty on the circus lot. Crowds of people pushed and shoved as we worked our way into the Big Top for the show. It is strange how things stick in a young person's mind but I can viv-idly remember the smells, the sounds and the sights we saw that day. The show started and the grand show opening parade made its way around the hippodrome track with animals draped with bright-colored trappings and the artists themselves dressed even better. It was a world of glitter and an awesome sight for a young man of six years to see! As the last elephant shuffled out of the big brown canvas tent and the parade was over, the ring-master, resplendent in a bright red coat, shiny black boots, white britches and wearing a tall stovepipe hat, blew his whistle to get the crowd's atten-tion.

"Ladies and gentlemen, I direct your attention to the big steel cage erected in the center ring." Suddenly spotlights came on illuminating the area. The ringmaster spoke again, this time enunciating every syllable as he announced in a loud voice, "The world's youngest and most fearless lion and tiger trainer—Mr. Clyde Beatty!"

Clyde Beatty saluted the audience, entered the big steel arena and did his act. The crowd cheered as Beatty put his animals through their tricks. Then, suddenly, one tiger jumped on another and ripped a long gash down his opponent's shoulder. The mele was a scene of utter confusion but Beatty eventually got them under control and managed to get all of the big cats back into their cages except the injured one. This one was lassoed, pulled over to the cage bars and the cut was drenched with what looked like tinc-ture of iodine. The tiger roared his disaproval—the crowd cheered!

Remembering all of this, I realized that was veterinary medicine as it was in those days. I hoped animal care had improved since then. The clanging bell of the street car jangled me out of my memories and at Neil Avenue I got off of the trolley and walked across the OSU Campus to my class.

Later in the summer, one evening after I got home from school, Mary Helen handed me the Columbus newspaper. It carried a full page advertisment about the Ringling Bros Barnum & Bailey Circus coming to Columbus. "Promise me," she said, "don't make any plans for that day." She insisted we go to the circus and meet her friend Ernestine who was now advertised as a star performer in that circus.

Circus day came and we rode the street car to the show grounds. I stared with amazement at the vast city of canvas, wagons and fascinating people. It was a world different from anything I had ever seen.

Taking my hand, my wife guided me past the front part of the circus to the "back yard." It was apparent she knew her way around and after finding someone who spoke English, we were directed to the Clarke dressing tent. Mrs. Clarke remembered Mary Helen and told us Ernestine was gone for the day but for us to come back to the evening show for a visit. Unfortunately I had to go back to school and besides, we didn't have enough money for a ticket!

That day the circus captured my attention like nothing I had ever seen before. We wandered around the lot and looked at the long line of elephants and brightly painted red wagons with the show's logo, "The Greatest Show On Earth," painted on each one. There were camels, acres of canvas with breeze-blown flags topping the center poles, and a lot of sleek, fat horses tied to a picket line behind the menagerie tent. In another tent, by themselves, was cage after cage of lions and tigers, all rumbling in talk only known to their kind. Added to this fascinating world were scores of noisy, laughing people, young and not so young, playing soccer in a vacant field behind the Big Top. The confusion of the foreign tongues and the sounds of the animals made the entire atmosphere a different world than what I had known. Little did I know someday some of these animals would be my patients and many of these people and their families would become our lifelong friends.

Mary Helen and I often talked about that day and later, after we graduated from college, she bought me a book, *Circus Doctor* written by Dr. J.Y. Henderson, chief veterinarian for the Greatest Show On Earth. This book soon earned priority space in my book case.

Henderson's book made me realize there was another side to veterinary medicine besides the run-of-the-mill domestic animal practice. I wondered at times what it would be like to give an elephant an injection of medicine or sew up a cut on a tiger or lion. I soon put these daydreams behind me, finished my education and we moved to Kentucky to practice.

The Ashland Oil & Refining Company is located here in Ashland. In those days, each year the company had a grand Christmas party with gifts for the employee's children and circus-type entertainment for "children of all ages." The show's producer, Jim Hetzer, was a friend and in the course of time, he invited Mary Helen and me to attend one of these parties. This invitation really started my circus involvement. Hetzer's productions consisted of only the very best acts of their type, and his cast of characters at all of his shows read like the "who's who" of show business. He was a talented man and produced nothing but quality entertainment.

Mary Helen and I met many people including great animal trainers such as Bucky Steele, a bear and elephant man, and Al Antonuci, a chimpanzee trainer. We also got to know many great show personalities including the fantastic clowns, Otto Griebling and Lou Jacobs. Steele became a good friend and, in a sense, was one of my first exotic animal clients. This whetted our appetite and the next step we took was to join the Circus Fans Association of America. We were on our way.

§   §   §

Clarksburg, West Virginia, hosted the circus fans' annual convention the next summer, and we paid our registration fees and made hotel reservations for our stay during the convention. Each year the circus fans were entertained by a different circus. This year Mill's Brothers' Circus, then out of Jefferson, Ohio, brought its show to West Virginia for the fans' entertainment. The Mills Brothers' Circus was a canvas show and a good one. Entertainment was their key note; compassion for their animals and their employees was one reason it was such a success.

We had a wonderful time there and before the convention was over, we knew everyone in the show. Capt. "Ky" Seagraves was the elephant trainer. After we were introduced, he looked surprised and said, "Doc, I'm out of Ashland too!" Incidentally, when you ask a circus person where he is from, the reply is always "out of," not "from." More new acquaintances included Rudy Docky the dog trainer, CoCo the clown and Victor Lewis, CoCo's clown act partner. CoCo acquainted us with his step-daughter Julia Drougett and her husband, both world class jugglers; Jon Zerbini, just out of France, with his lion act; and many other celebrities. Mr. Herman Joseph was an older clown whose career dated back to the very early part of the century. He and Mary Helen became great friends, corresponding on a regular basis until he died several years later. Jack, Jake and Harry Mills, the owners of the circus, also became our friends, as did Paul and Chris Hudson, the Pedrolas, and Roby and Paula Szoczy, to name just a few.

My circus veterinary career really started on the Mills show when

Seagraves, the elephant trainer, came to me and told me one of his animals was sick. "Doc," (we were on a first name basis already since we were both "out of" Ashland, Kentucky) "I got a bull we call India and she's got the chills. Gets 'em every once in a while and is sick for several days. I sure need your help." In the circus all elephants, regardless of sex, are called bulls. I was learning!

Now understand at that time I knew very little about elephants except they are big and they could hurt you if you weren't careful. Just by chance I had recently read a book written by an elephant man in Burma which mentioned some of the ailments he saw with his animals. One of the problems he described was a disease that caused chills. His suggested treatment was a pint of good gin!

I did some fast thinking and, for not really knowing what to do, I suggested Seagraves get a pint of whiskey and give India three fourths of it. I also told him to, "Check with me in an hour and let me know how she is."

Two hours later Captain Virgil Seagraves, an inebriated pachyderm master, came to me to report. "Doc, the bull is a lot better but I thought your recommended dose of whiskey was too much so I gave her only half the pint. I drank the rest of the booze myself." He recovered and so did India. This was my first elephant case. The same day Rudy Docky the dog trainer needed me, and what started as a fun vacation, ended up as another working day.

We visited Mills Bros. Circus at several of their stands during that summer, and every time we were on the show Mills had work for me to do. At the end of the show season Jack approached me and wondered if I would consider helping them when they had need for a veterinarian. He also suggested I come to winter quarters the next spring for the opening date. I jumped at the chance.

At the end of that same season, Mary Helen and I invited Victor Lewis, who was Harry Mills' brother-in-law, and CoCo to stop by the house for a short visit when they closed in Jefferson and were on their way to winter in Florida. They did just that, they stopped for a visit which lasted six months!

The next spring the show opened at Jefferson on a cold, snowy Easter weekend. *The Cleveland Plain Dealer* newspaper had publicized Mills Bros. Circus getting a new baby elephant. It also mentioned Jack Mills had Dr. Martin, an elephant specialist, on hand to examine the baby when it got there. I was more than flattered. Mary Helen and I went to Mills' winter quarters and we had no more than driven through the gates when Seagraves, Jack and Jake Mills met us. The baby elephant was sick. That night the poor little baby died of a painful abdominal condition in spite of my twelve-hour vigil and medical attention. That was my first circus animal loss. Jack and Jake thanked me for my effort and the animal was never mentioned again.

Over the next several years I did a lot of work for the Mills show and in a sense became part of the show itself. Eventually Mills took its Big Top down for the last time and that show closed. Some of the performers went to the Hoxie Bros. Circus which was for a time affiliated with Jack Mills. Many, including Paul and Chris Hudson, went to Sells and Gray, a new title managed by Bill English out of Sarasota, Florida. I followed Hudson and was their veterinarian for the years that Sells and Gray toured.

§   §   §

Ringling Bros. Barnum & Bailey Circus, the giant tent show I had seen in Columbus, Ohio, no longer existed under canvas after labor disputes forced the show to close in Pittsburgh in the mid-fifties. Now John North had his show in buildings and instead of the great railroad show it once was, it was now transported on trucks. Eventually they played Huntington, West Virginia. Mary Helen and I went to the circus hoping to meet Dr. J.Y. Henderson, chief veterinarian for the show and author of the book *Circus Doctor*. A midget clown showed us Henderson's trailer and I knocked on the door. A beautiful red-haired lady welcomed us to her home. A spontaneous friendship began and Dr. Henderson and his wife Martha became lifelong friends. During our visit I told him about my interest in performing animals, especially horses, and mentioned my limited experiences with the Mills circus. J.Y. and I hit it off right away. He was basically a horse man and when he heard about my horse background, our friendship was sealed. Before we left the show, he volunteered to help me any time I needed him and he promised someday he would come to our farm for a visit. He also wanted to know if I would be available to help him if the occasion came up. Of course I jumped at that chance too!

§ § §

Sells and Gray went out the next spring and I was on call as their animal doctor. Anna May, their favorite elephant, got sick in Indiana. I made a house call to see her. They had other animals too, including llamas, horses, the big cats and a camel named Tommy.

Camels are critters of their own world. When pushed too hard they spit at you. Ugh—the slimy stuff they regurgitate is awful when it hits you! They can also strike you with their front feet and kick harder than a mule with their hind feet. When everything goes their way, they are nice animals. Sells & Gray Circus's Tommy was no different than any other camel. He had his good days and his bad. Paul Hudson, the circus manager, called long distance one day and told me Tommy had a big knot on his jaw. The familiar saying, "Doc, come right away," concluded the phone call.

I drove to the show in southern Ohio and, sure enough, examination of Tommy revealed a large, hot, swollen jaw, obviously abcessed. Dave Mulaney was a friend of mine from previous circuses and on this show was Tommy's keeper. I looked at the swelling and even tried to feel the big lump, but Tommy did not cooperate. He swung his head in my direction and spat, trying his best to tell me to go away! Dave was holding the halter rope and only his quick action when he pulled Tommy's head aside from me kept me from getting soaked. Even though Tommy missed, I still felt sorry for him; it was obvious he was in pain. If I was going to open and drain the abscess, Tommy's restraint would be a problem. After a brief conversation, Dave and I decided to back the camel into a horse trailer and tie his head to the side. Recalling a time when I wormed a herd of elephants in another circus with medicine hidden in loaves of bread, we decided to divert him that way. Mulaney went to the cook house and got two loaves of white bread. He fed Tommy a slice. Tommy gulped it down. He fed him another slice and he gulped that one down too. I told Dave to keep feeding him the bread and when the time was right, I took my scalpel and made a neat incision at the bottom of the big lump. Tommy never objected, the abscess drained and Dave never stopped his bread anesthetic. Ingenuity saved the day. In a veterinarian's circus practice, ingenuity was involved in almost every case.

I followed Sells and Gray Circus for several years. Eventually they closed and I moved on to other shows.

§   §   §

One summer our daughter, Terri, went out on the Clyde Brothers Circus with the Lacy Troupe rolling globe act who were her friends from the old Mills show. Clyde Brothers toured the Midwest and toward the end of the summer, Mary Helen and I drove to Deadwood, South Dakota, to pick Terri up and bring her back to Kentucky in time for school to start. We stayed on with the show three weeks and most of the time was spent treating animals. I wormed the big elephants, treated the five baby elephants for sunburn, castrated two baby bears for Wally Naughton and discussed management problems with Cimone about his chimpanzees. Terri worked for Billy and Gee Gee Powell who had an outstanding dog act and also had the cotton candy concession. Terri soon earned the title of the "Cotton Candy Queen." It was a holiday turned into a working trip.

By this time my reputation was growing as an exotic animal veterinarian with a specialty in circus work. It was very different kind of veterinary practice. In all cases I maintained my office in Ashland and simply made "house calls" when I was needed. Sometimes though, I would be gone for several days at a time! Besides Clyde Brothers Circus, I was called to other shows such as Fisher Brothers Circus, Clark and Walters show, and Ringling Brothers, Barnum & Bailey Circus. Dr. Henderson, Ringling's veterinarian, helped me with his knowledge and experience. When I had something different, I called him and we talked it out together.

At the same time I was going out with these shows, many of the circus animal owners came to the clinic with their problems. Charley Allen and his family spent several weeks with us while they were between dates. They had a zebra, dogs and bears. Charley was an excellent trainer and worked in Hollywood in the movies training animals. While they were staying at the clinic I castrated a bear for him which later starred in the TV series, *Gentle Ben*. When the show was aired my friends joked the reason Ben was so gentle was that, "Doc Martin had a sharp knife!"

It was not uncommon for big trucks carrying wild animals to park in my lot at the clinic. The neighbors soon learned that it was everyday business and often never bothered to see what had been shipped to me for treatment. A man in Florida shipped a South American Jaguar and an African Leopard to me for surgery. It was no problem as I had a squeeze cage designed and built just to handle such cases. Bucky Steele, whom I met on the Ashland Oil Company Christmas show, was a frequent visitor, bringing his bears, lions and a tiger. One morning Bucky came to me for some health certificates needed to take his elephants into Canada. He had eleven huge pachyderms lined up in my front yard. That day all the neighborhood was present!

My telephone stayed busy with show people wanting veterinary advice. I gave it freely and still do to this day. At the same time I stayed in contact with Henderson and he too soon became a regular visitor there in the clinic, helping me with my work. We were a good team, and, at the time, dominated the circus aspect of veterinary medicine.

§   §   §

Ringling Brothers, Barnum & Bailey Circus—called the "Big One" by many—had overcome its hard times and was now back on the road as a railroad show. Irvin Feld and his associates remodeled the circus and it was once again truly, "The Greatest Show On Earth." Winter quarters was in Venice, Florida, and all preparation, rehearsals, equipment repairs and other arrangements for the upcoming season were conducted there. In 1963, Dr. Henderson called me and suggested I come visit him and go with the show on the Florida dates—Venice, Tampa, Miami and Jacksonville. He said he would appreciate my help. I almost shouted, "Yes," at his invitation.

J.Y. and Mrs. Henderson lived in Sarasota and met me at the airport. Early the next morning as we drove to Venice, J.Y. talked to me about a lame horse that concerned him. He explained the horse was used in a bareback riding act owned by the Stephenson family and the slight lameness made the animal at times unusable. He described the symptoms and almost at once I thought I knew what ailed this horse. As soon as we got onto the grounds, I was introduced to Frank Stephenson and his family. They brought the horse from the stable, I did my examination and confirmed what I thought was a joint inflammation, or simple arthritis. I asked Dr. Henderson if he had a certain cortisone-like drug used commonly for arthritis and inflamed joints. He did and sent one of his grooms to the veterinary wagon for the medicine and a syringe. I injected the medicine into the horse's leg joint, told Mr. Stephenson to lead his horse off at a trot and in about a minute the lameness was gone! Frank Stephenson was amazed at the spontaneous results and at once I was his horse expert! Then I realized I had made one of the most embarrassing mistakes of my life. In my eagerness to help, I had belittled my veterinary friend in the eyes of one of his circus co-workers. Properly I should have discussed the case first and told J.Y. what I thought he should do and let him do the work. The damage was done and it concerned me deeply. I am quite sure Henderson never realized my concern, or for that matter ever gave the incident any thought but from that time on. I always stayed in the background until we discussed our case.

The Stephensons were from Ireland, originating from a circus family of many generations. Besides having a high class riding act, they also had the finest dog act of the era. They are some of the finest people I have ever met and Mary Helen and I are proud to know them and consider them our friends. Over the years our farm, Jomar, became a retirement home for their horses. Two of the ring horses and one pony are buried at Jomar.

Circus veterinary practice is not the exciting career my friends think it is. Most of the work was preventive medicine and proper animal management. Circus animals are well cared for and as a rule no expense is spared when it comes to their health and nutrition. Contrary to what the animal rights advocates declare, in most cases the animals are not mistreated but are handled with respect and compassion. Training is done with rewards for conditioned reflexes the trainer uses to his advantage. Punishment is not part of the program; it just isn't good judgment to have a wild tiger or a great big elephant hold a grudge against its trainer!

Ingenuity played a major part in my practice with the circus. Mrs. Rhodin had a beautiful white stallion she rode in a center ring dressage performance. This horse was her pride and joy and she was at my side every time any little thing happened to her "Baby." On the show, in the animal tent, the horses are tied to a picket line that extends from one end of the tent to the other. Generally nothing separates one horse from another. Most animals are content this way and cause no trouble. At the time of this particular incident, however, most of the horses on the show were stallions and all stallions, or studs as they are usually called, tend to bite.

One morning the stud tied next to Baby managed to take a good bite at his fancy neighbor, causing a cut about four inches long under the mane on Baby's neck. Henderson was not there and one of the grooms came to me, all excited, and said Mrs. Rhodin would kill us both if she knew her horse had been hurt. I agreed—he was probably right. I cleaned up the wound, which by now had quit bleeding, and sutured the skin together. It was a nice neat job but one I am sure would have shocked the prima donna horse lady. Red, the groom, and I tried every way we could to brush the mane over the cut but it still showed. While Red and I were thinking about our problem, one of my clown friends, Mark Anthony, walked by the tent and gave me a cheery "good morning." In a mental flash I had the answer. I stopped him and asked him if he would give me some of his clown white grease paint. With a big clown smile he said, "Yes, does this make me a real Doc?" and he trotted over to clown alley, got into his trunk and in just a minute or two was back with a big jar of white zinc oxide. It was the best thing in the world for this situation. He and Red and I smeared the white salve all over the repaired cut, and the show went on. Mrs. Rhodin never knew anything about the injury until after her act was over. And then, after she recovered her composure, and with my assurance that the cut would heal with no complications, she thanked me.

In my show business career I treated many different kinds of animals for many different ailments. Chimpanzees needed teeth extracted, elephants needed toe nails trimed, and sore-legged horses needed my expertise and my horse liniments. Dog act people had their problems and I tended their animals too. The human animal also had my attention! Trapeze stars often came to me for liniment and consoling words. J.Y. and I, maybe overstepping our bounds, doled out aspirin and antibiotic pills for those with colds and minor ailments. Cuts and bruises were routine treatment in both man and beast in my circus practice.

Over a period of several years I was on and off of the Ringling show, sometimes Henderson was there and other times I filled his shoes when he was gone. Traveling on the circus train to different cities, the pleasant, and sometimes unpleasant, experiences along with the fascinating people in the show became part of my life. The circus world is hard for an outsider to get into, but I was accepted as one of them and to this day have the show people's respect and friendship. These were exciting and rewarding times, but in retrospect I am not sure I wanted a permanent position with one show. My reputation was well established and my circus house calls, if you want to call them that, were the envy of most animal doctors. I had the best of both worlds—when my work was done, it was nice to say goodbye to the spangles and sawdust and go home to Kentucky and the critters and the people in the hills.

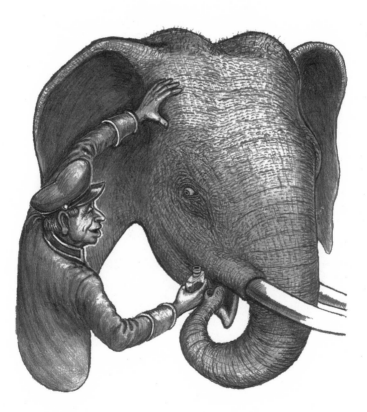

CATS AND DOGS AND OTHER THINGS

I N SPITE OF THE HOOPLA, SPANGLES AND COTTON CANDY, MINI-ADVENTURES with horses, itchy tigers, sick elephants, nasty camels and pigs and cows, the mainstay of my professional career had to be my small animal practice and the Martin Veterinary Clinic.

The idea of my clinic developed while I was still a student in the university. There I had visions of an ultramodern, state-of-the-art veterinary hospital where I imagined myself performing miraculous healings and doing fine surgery on both large and small animals. At that time there were few institutions like my imaginary one except in the veterinary colleges or maybe the biggest cities. It was a far-fetched dream, but somehow I never lost the idea and knew sooner or later I would have such a facility.

Telephones and paved roads eventually became a part of eastern Kentucky. World War II was behind us and social and economic recovery was evident everywhere. My town in particular did well. Unemployment was low and industry—the Ashland Oil Company, Armco Steel and the C&O Railroad—employed most of the men and women. Unlike some of the other river towns, people were busy and seemed to have money to spend. I began to fit into this picture and was determined to develop my practice and the ideas about my clinic.

Construction began in 1952 and the clinic opened a year later. The main building had my private office, an examination room, pharmacy area, waiting room, and a surgery designed to handle large animal cases as well as small animal operations. A sophisticated—for the time—X-ray room, a large kennel room and a set of outside exercise runs completed the unit. The second building was a barn for large animal patients. It was airy and easy to keep and manage. I extended an open invitation to anyone who wanted to visit and see how we proposed to handle our patients and animal visitors. The response to my invitation was amazing: many curious people came to look at my new innovation in animal care. Most everyone was impressed and it was interesting to hear the comments. I overheard one man tell his wife he thought, "the Doctor is crazy—who's going to spend big money on a cat or a dog to pay for this?" Other remarks were more favorable. The most gratifying to me were the comments about our management and I was pleased when I heard, "Dr. Martin's clinic is squeaky clean." And squeaky clean it was and squeaky clean it stayed all of the years I practiced.

As money allowed I bought equipment I thought I needed, including the first oxygen system and the first ultrasound generator in any veterinary clinic in Kentucky. Almost from the beginning there was constant change, enlarging or adding on, building new cages or renovating old ones and creating new facilities to fit the times. It was like Topsy in the story of Uncle Tom's Cabin, it "jest growed!" Now, nearly fifty years later, the clinic still functions and even though I no longer own it, the Martin Veterinary Clinic is still there serving the community. Perhaps this is some sort of a monument to me. If so, I am grateful. But bricks and stones and all the nice things are not what this story is about. It is still a story about eastern Kentucky and the hill country people.

To recap events from earlier years, a declining large animal population and my back injury acquired on Chris Crank's farm, made me decide to give up my large animal practice. The farm calls and the stockyard work went first. I continued treating horses but an old allergy seemed to accelerate and suddenly every time I examined a horse I would sneeze and break out in a skin rash! The critter that started it all—the horse—had done me in! My decision was made; I would restructure my practice and my clinic would become a small-animal facility. In my mind I could see a long range program which included a trained staff of capable assistants and a state-of-the-art diagnostic laboratory. However, the wanderlust, the adventure, the excitement and the glitter of the exotic animals and show business was still in my blood and I did retain my circus practice.

During the course of a conversation with one of Mary Helen's friends, I was told most people never brought their pets to me because I was never in the clinic when they needed me. Now that situation changed. Soon the word was out that I didn't do large animal work anymore. The small animal business boomed. It was indeed a different work world I now lived in.

On the plus side were the regular work hours. We opened at seven in the morning and closed for supper at five in the evening. For a few years I went back to the clinic and conducted night office hours until eight o'clock. A typical day was fun, sometimes even better than the circus! Over the course of time I saw sick dogs, sick cats, pet birds, gerbils, ferrets and snakes and any other kind of animal you could make a pet out of. Most of my patients were cats and the dogs and their problems were handled well, thanks to modern veterinary medicine and the skill and compassion of my good employees.

One of my biggest assets began when Stormy Lemaster came to me and applied for a job. Stormy was about my age, wore a pleasant smile under a head-full of red hair. He also had one shirt sleeve safety-pinned up over an arm that was not there. In our initial interview, he admitted to less than a high school education and told me he originated in the hill country—"up Sandy"—near Salyersville, close to Hell's Acre. I didn't know where that was but I assumed it had to be some mystical part of the hills of Appalachia. "I came down here to make myself better." He also told me he was a hard worker and thought he would be an asset to my practice. In my mind I just couldn't imagine a one-armed man doing what I wanted him to do until he said, "Doctor Martin, I like animals and I think I will like this work. If you employ me I will do the best I can for you and," he went on to say, "I can do anything you ask me to do except wheel a wheelbarrow!" Quite a statement for a person who lost his arm in an industrial accident. True to his word, Stormy never let me down. Our association lasted over twenty years until he decided to leave and open a pet shop. He was successful there too.

I also give credit to another long-time employee, Earl Hardin. Earl was born and reared in sight of the Catlettsburg stockyard and like most kids spent all of his spare time working in the sales barn. This made him particularly good with the large animals. But he was equally adept with the cats and dogs. Without him, after Stormy left my employ, the practice would have faltered. Earl became a very good surgical assistant and together we developed a team pattern not generally found in a situation like ours. Eventually Earl left me too, but not before I made a decision that was a big factor in the new look of the Martin Veterinary Clinic—I decided to use nothing but female employees.

About the time I decided to make these changes, the veterinary technician program started. Most veterinarians were plagued by phone calls and literature from the colleges who offered this program, wanting us to employ their graduates. We, practicing doctors, had no idea what these people could do and we had no idea how much money they expected. Most of us had seen hard times and it didn't seem right to pay someone else for services we could do for ourselves. Eventually, not thinking much of the idea, I let those thoughts slip my mind.

On a cold winter day I got a phone call from a lady asking me if I would give her granddaughter a job. Now if *I* was looking for work, I would go ask for it myself. "Doctor Martin, I know this is a strange request but after the big blizzard we just had, my granddaughter is snowed-in at college and can't get to town to talk to you. I'm applying for her."

Well, I knew this lady, Gypsy Hughes was her name, and I said, "Gypsy, tell her to come on up here as soon as the snow melts and I'll give her an interview." The girl came a week later and I gave her a job. That turned out to be a banner day and after seeing what she could do with an animal and seeing the potential she had to help my practice, I was sold on the technician program. This young lady, Katherine Hughes, was the first of three college-graduated veterinary technicians I employed.

The ladies were dedicated and exhibited more compassion for the animals and for the clients themselves than their male counterparts. The clients seemed to appreciate female help and be more at ease with the girls, particularly in emotion-filled times with their pets.

Besides Katherine, I eventually employed Hart Cruise, a gung-ho technician from Lexington, Kentucky, and Lisa Hahn, a West Virginia native. I also staffed my kennel with two ladies. Teresa Broughton and Becky Murphy were blessings and along with the rest of the staff we had a team that was hard to beat. Now some twelve years after I left the practice, Becky and Teresa are still there working for Doctor Gary Duncan, the young DVM who bought my practice.

Early in the practice I had the fortune—good or bad—to meet just about everybody in the entire area. Some were acquaintances only as clients; others became part of our lifestyle and activities after hours. We were invited to parties and to other social events but it was hard to make firm commitments to these gatherings because of the long uncertain hours I worked. Then when we did get to those, I remember one of Mary Helen's friends asking her how she managed to stay around me after handling all those "old dirty cows and cats and dogs?" We were invited to join the country club but had neither time nor money for that program. Our city has a nice country club and its membership includes most of the good business people and of course the usual social climbers. We never did join and looking back over all of the years without it, I am glad we never belonged. But all of these people soon became my clients with their dogs and cats, cattle and horses and other animals. On the not-so-social list were my good farmer clients who also had their dogs and cats and made my clinic part of their routine. So Mary Helen and I had a choice of friends, and we made that choice and fit ourselves into a mixture that included some from every walk of life.

The combination of this new concept of an animal hospital, the addition of the professionally trained technicians, our acquired social and business-associated friends, plus my reputation as a good veterinarian, caused the system to work. Once again, I moved to meet the challenge of a new era.

The transition from a general practice to a strictly small animal practice was slow. The farmers still came for advice and my help. I did my best to serve them until they found another veterinarian or other ways. The transition was hard and the last two large animal calls I ever made were adventures in themselves.

§   §   §

Roy "Cold Water" Hutchison was a regular client. He raised cows, some pigs and chickens, and a big family of boys and girls up in Rock House "holler" just on the west side of the county. Cold Water was a fireman on the railroad and supposedly earned his nickname because he was too lazy to keep the fires stoked and fueled in the big railroad steam engines. Now I don't really know if he was lazy, because every time I dealt with him, he seemed to have a scheme of some sort going to generate money. One hot spring day he came into the office walking with a crutch to help him manipulate a huge plaster of paris cast that started at his very dirty foot and extended up to his waist. It appeared obvious that with that much of a plaster cast he must have a badly broken leg! He managed the crutch with one hand and with the other he was dragging an old hound dog along on a rope. The hound was covered with fleas, its skin scratched raw and was covered with some filthy, greasy substance that made noticeable streaks on my clean floor as he dragged the dog into my examining room. The dog was a mess and before I could ask Cold Water what was on his hound, he told me he had already treated his dog with used motor oil.

"Roy, why in the hell motor oil?"

"'cause it is the bestus way to cure the mange."

"I don't think the mange is this dog's problem. Dirt and fleas are the culprits. Look here, there's thousands of fleas on this poor old hound!" Mentally I started to itch just at the sight of all those parasites!

"Well, John," he called me always by my name, "I just knowed everybody used old motor oil on their itchin' dogs and I was jest tryin' to save me some money doing your job for ya. And besides, the old dog ain't the reason I come here anyways. What I really need is some little bull calves made into steers before they git so big we can't handle 'em."

"You know I'm not doing that kind of work anymore." He acted like he never heard me.

"Don't you worry none, th' kids 'ill be there to hep us."

I gave in, sighed and said, "OK, leave the dog here and I'll come to your place in the morning. Be sure you have the calves penned up." Somehow I just knew in my mind these were not little, as he said, bull calves. "By the way, Roy, how did you break your leg?"

"I slipped and fell off of the locomotive. I'm a thinkin' I'm agoin' to sue the railroad." He hobbled out the door on his crutch, dragging his heavy plaster cast. I sent the dog to my helper for soap and water and a flea dip.

The next morning I drove out to the Hutchison place and sure enough penned in a small corral at the barn were six or seven big bull calves, already twice as big as Roy told me they were. The pen was a solid mass of mud and cow manure, deep enough to be over the knees of these half-grown bulls. A swarm of flies hovered like a cloud over the entire barn lot.

I knew right then I was in for a real hassle before my day was done and, smiling to myself, I thought about Mary Helen's party friend asking about how she stood it with her husband associating with "those old dirty cows, cats and dogs."

Roy yelled to two of his boys, "Come here and grab one of them calves and hold 'em so John here can put the clamps on him." Reluctantly the biggest boy climbed over the fence and sank knee deep in the filth. He grabbed the smallest calf and somehow I managed to make a steer out of that animal. The next calf was bigger and the kid couldn't hold it, so Roy, now mad at his offspring's help, let out an oath and after dropping his crutch, climbed over the board fence into the cow lot and helped me. He grabbed the largest calf and somehow managed to hold it while I did my job. Together we made steers out of the rest of the young bulls, me on my two good legs and Roy slipping and sliding in the mud and cow manure with his supposedly broken leg! After we were finished, he climbed the fence again, sat down on the ground and with his pocket knife scraped the filth off of his cast. Then he stood up, shook his lame leg and wiggled his toes to get rid of the rest of the mud and manure. Finally he picked up his crutch and said, "John, let's go to the house and eat."

I thought I would get sick right on the spot. I was covered with cow manure, mud and all other kinds of barnyard dirt, hot and ready for a bath. "Gosh, Roy, I'd like to stay, but I got another appointment." That was the fastest excuse I could come up with to get out of there. "But if you don't mind, I would like to have some soap and a pan of water so I can clean myself up before I go back to the office—I've got a lot of work to do." Mrs. Hutchison produced an old porcelain dishpan full of warm water, a bar of Lifebuoy Soap and some rags to dry on. The pungent Lysol fragrance of the Lifebuoy was just barely enough to overcome the barnyard smell. I collected my money and drove down Rock House Road until I was out of sight and stopped the car. I took off my filthy clothes and drove almost naked to my house. There I stood in a wonderful hot shower until all signs of Cold Water's bulls were washed away.

Three days later Roy called me again and wanted me to come look at a cow he thought had been struck by lightning. He needed a letter from me indicating lightning was the cause of death so he could collect from the insurance company. When I got to the farm, sure enough, the cow was lying with her head across a wire fence, dead and bloated. But something wasn't just right—there were skid marks in the grass indicating the cow had either been dragged to the fence or, in her last throes of death staggered into the wire herself from way up on the side of the hill. I told Roy I couldn't sign any certificate like he wanted and uttered, "I don't see the usual burn marks like lightning makes when it hits 'em." And then, continuing my examination, just by luck I found a bullet hole in her hide. Someone had shot his cow, then she staggered down the hill and fell on the fence. My statement was made to that effect.

Cold Water Hutchison was a good client. His hound dog got well and he sold his steers that fall at the market for a good price. I don't know if he ever collected his insurance money, but he was always good to me and certainly entertaining. Roy was truly a friend and a good man in spite of his lifestyle and character. His constant bragging about me and my new clinic was a real plus; perhaps he was paying me back for the cow with the bullet hole in her and the day we clamped all of those filthy bull calves. Best of all, his kids grew up and have done well. I am proud to have known him and I still see some of the family occasionally.

§   §   §

One evening just before closing time, my friend Charles Montague was in the office discussing an insurance policy we were considering changing. Our business didn't take long to conclude and as he started towards the door he turned and asked, "Doc, just what are you going to do when you give up all of this fun stuff with cows and pigs and horses?" Then he added, "Just what am I going to do for entertainment?"

I laughed, "Charles, I'm going to sleep late and go to bed early. I think I have earned some rest. Go find your entertainment with your steamboats and steam engines—I'm through!" The phone rang before Montague could make any comment.

I picked it up and a squeaky voice said, "Doctor Martin, this is Farmer Picklesiemer—would you please . . . " Farmer, and that was his real name, was always polite, thanking me and saying please and asking forgiveness if he hindered me. "I need you to attend one of my cows that's trying to come fresh." He meant by this remark she was trying to deliver her calf. "I know you are trying to quit but come this one last time, please." Charles didn't know who was calling, but I could see a great big grin come over his face and he knew it was a farmer calling for help. He also figured I just couldn't say no!

Admitting temporary defeat, I said, "OK, Farmer, I'll be out there right away." Picklesiemer lived at the edge of town, not three miles from the office.

"Well, Doc," Montague whined, "I'll just have to go with you and see you don't get hurt." He laughed as he made his joke. We got into my car and drove to Farmer's barn. Picklesiemer was a short-statured, thin man that farmed some prime land facing on the main federal highway. Farmer was a frugal man with a dollar, had a thin faced wife and a young daughter who worked hard on the farm helping him raise a few first-class Hereford cattle. Not to discredit him, he was a hard worker, but his twangy voice and his skimpy ways with money made him a character to be reckoned with.

By the time Charles and I got there, it was pitch dark. Farmer was waiting, standing in the doorway of the barn bathed in the weak light of a single electric bulb dangling from a wire in the barn loft.

A great big Hereford cow was tied to a post in the aisle of the barn. She was alternately straining, resting and chewing her cud and then straining again. With every uterine contraction, she bellowed with pain. Her calf just didn't seem to want to enter our world. Farmer had hot water, towels and soap ready. He and I had been through this several times before and he pretty well knew the routine.

I scrubbed the cow's rear end and tied her tail around to her side out of my way, put on my obstetrical sleeve and began my work. Charles already had the delivery instruments in the bucket of water with some disinfectant. Over the years he had become a pretty good cow mid-wife! Examination revealed the calf was coming backwards, nothing unusual or hard since this cow had delivered several calves in her lifetime. When I tried to position the calf's legs so I could get the obstetrical chains on them, she humped up, gave a mighty contraction and fell down — my arm up inside her womb clear to my shoulder. When she fell, my backbone popped like a gun and I went down with her! Somehow I managed to get up and the cow did too. I didn't know who was in worse shape—the poor cow or the poor doctor trying to help her. Finally we delivered the calf and I managed to hobble back to the car. Farmer Picklesiemer was generous with his apologies, satisfied that his prize cow would be alright, but grimaced when he handed me a well-worn ten dollar bill for my work and my pain!

Back at my car I said, "Charles, if you don't mind, drive me back to the office. I can manage to make it home from there."

Serious as he could be he replied, "Hell, Doc, when I made that remark about keeping you from gettin' hurt, I was just funnin' you." I accepted his condolences and his Kentucky colloquialisms. Later, as the pain went away, I looked back over a long friendship and some exciting times with Charles. I know he misses our trips together and so do I. We still see each other often, and now, years after this all happened, he never fails to recall and relive one or more of our farm visits.

That was the last farm call I ever made. My back eventually got better and for all of the years I practiced after that episode, I never picked up anything, not even a small cat or dog!

§   §   §

Small animal practice was much different than the farm and large animal work. On the plus side, the facilities at hand made it possible to practice better medicine. The availability of the diagnostic laboratory and the trained technicians confirmed conclusions whereas on the farm they were often just assumed. Clean white clinic coats replaced the heavy rubber boots and coveralls of the farm doctor and, best of all, the working hours were more regulated—albeit a twelve hour, or longer, day was not unusual. X-ray and surgical facilities, gas anesthetic machines and up-to-date modern equipment made a different work world. Now instead of dirt floors and chickens competing for space in my barnyard operating room and with newspapers covering the operating sites, there were sterile surgical drapes, proper lights and immaculate surroundings.

The client's needs were different. The small animal owner didn't depend on his or her pet for family subsistence as the farmer did with his animals. Consequently, the pet owner generally had more love and compassion for the animals. There was a sense of family bonding and pride of ownership I didn't see with the farmer. This doesn't mean farmers mistreated or disliked their animals, but as a rule the farm animal was a tool of the trade, a means to an end, a commodity for the farmer's survival. Only in a few cases was the pet, "Just there for the kids."

The business aspect of such an operation was as different as day and night. Instead of being the sole operator, now I employed several people and began to experience the woes and problems of a big business, paying the salaries, the bills and collecting the money for services rendered.

On the negative side were some of the idiosyncrasies of the people. Most were nice and appreciated my work. I made many life-long friends, and when I eventually retired, they sincerely thanked me for what I had done for them. Some had no real bond to any doctor and bounced around from veterinarian to veterinarian to suit their own pattern or simply to hunt for money bargains. It was very disheartening to see a client drive into the parking lot in a fancy, high-priced automobile and then want to charge my services or want to know, "Why do you charge so much?" Money was hard to collect from quite a few, especially some of the supposedly affluent. In my practice they earned the name, "nickel millionaires." Some of the people were nasty, or should I say, we had a personality clash. As the years went by, some of these people really got to me and finally, I told them not to come back. I only regret I did not do it sooner! But in spite of the ups and downs of a small animal hospital, there was never a dull moment and no two cases were ever alike.

§ § §

Not every day was full of story-telling happenings. Most days were devoted to giving "shots," spaying cats and dogs and neutering male animals. Broken bones were common and most veterinarians became very adept at fracture repair. Advances in veterinary orthopedics were rapid. We used bolts and nuts, screws, rods and wires to fix breaks long before our counterpart MDs made it routine.

An interesting sidelight to my fracture repair technique came years later when my wife fell on the ice and fractured her right arm in several places. Dr. Robert Love was my preference for the attending orthopedic surgeon and while we were in the emergency room looking at the initial X-rays, he turned to me and said, "Dr. Martin, this is a complicated case; I am fortunate to have a veterinarian here to assist me!" I appreciated his comment, and his humor at a stressful time, and pleased he recognized the capabilities of my profession. Of course Dr. Love managed to repair Mary Helen's discomforts without my help. He is a fantastic technician, did a remarkable job and pleased me when he admitted we veterinarians led the way to human orthopedics.

Other surgical procedures were equally as rewarding and technical as bone repair. Routinely we performed tendon repairs, removed tumors and patched up cuts and other wounds. Dental disease prevention and small animal dentistry played a big role in the day-by-day practice. Corrective surgery, such as removal of bladder stones in both dogs and cats, a fairly common operation, was spectacular to the owner when he saw the cup full of stones we sometimes removed. Caesarean Sections to deliver new-born were common place, particularly in the large headed dogs like the Boston Terriers, Pekingese and Pugs. Elective surgery such as tail docking and ear cropping was in great demand.

Not all of my clinic work was surgery. Sick cats and dogs filled my office hours each day. As the practice got older, and me too, I saw less old-time runny-nosed, mattery-eyed Distemper and after the huge Rabies epidemics years earlier, I saw no more cases of that horrible disease. Vaccines protecting the animal from these diseases had been improved tremendously, as had client education to have them given. As the older diseases seemed to disappear, new maladies began to show up. Heart worm, in both dogs and cats, rapidly covered the country. It was transmitted by the mosquito and migrated from the swamps of the South to the far reaches of Upper Michigan, New England and even Canada. In a few short years, heart worm became a common name among pet owners. The advent of air transportation of animals probably accelerated the spread of some of these diseases. Then came Lyme Disease. This was another parasite-vectored disease, this one transmitted by the deer tick. This disease became serious when it was determined humans could be infected as well as dogs and cats. Routine ear infections and other common diseases were commonplace. The small animal clinic was a busy place with full surgical loads scheduled every day as well as a never-ending variety of illnesses in many different breeds of animals.

§   §   §

But not all of the discomfort involved the animals. The veterinarian and his helpers occasionally suffered too, not only from the possibility of infectious disease, but from discomforts caused by the client.

Some owners purposely never told me the animal's symptoms! I guess they figured it was my job to find out what was wrong. These same people, wanting me to believe they were real dog experts, offered their opinions and at the same time even told me how they would treat the case! Some times the client would liven things up when he talked about the "dumb vet" he had taken his dog to just before he came to me! They often discussed their home-made treatments and one even informed me he knew how to cure all of these cases. I had been through one of these sessions one day and as the dog owner was ready to leave, he asked me again if I knew what I was doing was the best for his dog. To add insult to an already suffering animal doctor, these types invariably wanted to know why I charged so much for my work! Days like this caused me to have a lousy sense of humor.

A few of my clients were always inconsiderate and were a constant source of irritation. My parking lot never was big enough, even though I had paved it and increased the size two times over the years. One short, fat, over-girdled woman who wore her hair piled up seven or eight inches over the top of her head was the worst offender. She always managed to park her big Lincoln in three parking places and when I asked her why, when others were waiting in the street for a spot, she replied, "Why should I bother? Those people can figure out their own way!"

"Ma'am, that's not really very considerate of you and sure deprives some-one else a place to park."

She glared at me and walked out in a huff. Her last remarks as she waggled her head and waddled toward the door were, "Well I never. You are so rude!" I didn't appreciate her comments but I did appreciate her leaving.

In every veterinary practice, sooner or later little wild animals are pre-sented. Usually they are baby rabbits, injured birds or sometimes even snakes! Wounded owls and even hawks came to me and over the years I saw several deer patients. It was my policy to treat these patients as best I could at no charge. The short fat lady with the big car which took up several spaces in my parking lot was one of these who brought me wild creatures. She always managed to come in at inopportune times with a crippled starling, a baby squirrel or an orphaned baby robin. I gave her full attention and was se-cretly pleased that my expertise worked with the wild critters too. One day, after the parking lot episode, she brought in a baby starling with a broken wing. I fixed it as best I could with adhesive tape and toothpick splints. I will admit it wasn't a pretty repair, but it was serviceable and with the woman's attention I figured the bird would recover. When I finished my wild-bird-orthopedics and handed the bird back to her, she made the remark, "Your work certainly isn't very pretty."

A serge of adrenalin flooded all through me and I am sure my blood pressure went way up! I took a deep breath, tried to control myself, and finally I asked her, "Why do you come to me if you don't appreciate what I do for you?"

She never hesitated a second. "You are the cheapest vet in town."

I had had it and in no uncertain terms I told her to leave and never come back. Once again she stared at me and said, "Well I never. You are so rude!" This time I appreciated her remarks.

Some of my other clients thought they knew how to beat the game too. They managed to come during our lunch break and insisted we put down our sandwich and care for them "before the crowd came." We learned to combat these types and never answered the bell until exactly when office hours started. A few others played it the other way, they waited until the last scheduled minute and them waltzed in and dragged our day out, sometimes for an hour or more! These were selfish, self-serving people.

Of course there were those who let their dogs urinate or defecate on the floor and never had the courtesy to take the dog outside or even offer to help clean it up. Certainly they never considered me or the other people patiently waiting to see me.

Some not only brought the cat or dog to the clinic but also their kids and usually some borrowed ones from the neighbors too. After all, one lady told me, every kid is nuts about cats and dogs!

Some of the most provoking incidents involved money and my professional fees. A few of the old-timers occasionally let me know they thought I was robbing them and reminded me what I charged back in the early fifties! Some also reminded me they had sent many clients my way and suggested I consider that when I made my charges. Then there were those that made all kind of excuses such as a sick mother-in-law, high car payments, cost of vacations and other bills. Then one lady mentioned that the vet is a luxury and she always stuck my bill on the bottom of the pile. It was a tussle but in the long run I never lost very much money and in the long run I also was really appreciated by those that were the very first "to cast stones."

Although not frequent, many of these incidents wore on me and my family. Telephone calls at all hours of the day and night wanting free advice were a plague. It was not unusual for the phone to ring maybe three or four times after we had gone to bed. Finally I did the unthinkable. I had an unlisted telephone put in at home! Every doctor in town said it wouldn't work, but I know they were jealous because I had the nerve to do it. It did work, and it was wonderful to be relieved of the nagging, meaningless phone calls that came all night long. Of course my good clients all had the number, or if I sent a pet home that would possibly need my services, that owner always had the number too. I still have an unlisted number, even though these days it makes no difference, but it does screen the salesman, phone promoters and agitators. Now I sleep all night long without interruption.

§   §   §

Almost every day there was one glitch or another to break the routine. Mrs. Andre is a good client, but sometimes self-serving. Her case is typical of what I am talking about.

It's ten minutes before closing time and the telephone is ringing again. The telephone has had a very busy day. Hart, one of the technicians answers it and I hear her say, "Martin Veterinary Clinic," then a pause while she listens to the caller's comments. "Yes, Mrs. Andre, we still close at five o'clock." Another pause and Hart answers reluctantly, "We will wait for you, but please hurry. The doctor has a firm appointment out of the office at six."

This routine is not unusual in my clinic and probably many like it.

Mrs. Andre, the caller, is a busy lady but her business always seems to get to us at closing time. Nevermind, she has two dogs and a big old tomcat we all like. And she is a good client. A few minutes later she shows up. The patient this time is her cat. The tomcat has a very unique name—Tom!

She puts Tom on the examination table. It is obvious he is very sick. Before I can question her about Tom's symptoms, she says, "Dr. Mawtin," she was from New Jersey and didn't pronounce her Rs too well, "He sits in the littah box and strains. His bowels don't move and he acts like he's constipated. I just don't understand it, I gave him the cat laxative yestaday and the day befoah that too!"

Now I know this cat has been sick longer than Mrs. Andre says and she has tried everything she knew how to do. I am her last resort. That's OK with me—we get paid for that service.

I get my thermometer and start to take his temperature. Of course any animal is fidgety when you insert a thermometer into his rectum! Tom shows his reluctance. He squalls like the Devil himself is chasing him and tries to escape by climbing up Mrs. Andre's sweater. His claws are imbedded in her clothes and from the grimace on her face, some are imbedded in her skin too! She is screaming at me—her East Coast accent completely gone now—"What have you done to him? He's awful. He's never like this at home."

Disturbed by my insinuation of wrong, I answer, "Mrs. Andre, I haven't even touched him. He is sick, in a strange place and he is scared. Let me have him."

Hart helps—freeing first one claw filled foot, then another, guides Tom from Mrs. A's shoulder and the cat, still squalling and scratching, is finally deposited on my exam table. The rectal thermometer, after a little lubrication, finally finds its way and I slide my hand under his belly to feel what I suspected—a hard, fully distended urinary bladder. Tom has what we call in the profession FUS—abbreviation for Feline Urinary Syndrome. Tom's temperature is just slightly elevated which is probably what is expected in stressful situation like this.

"Lady, your cat has a blocked urethra. He can't urinate and that is why he is straining. He's real sick and is suffering uremic poisoning. He requires immediate attention." I paused for just a minute to allow my comments to sink in. "These cases are real emergencies."

"OK, Doctor, give him some medicine and I'll take him home."

"It isn't that easy. First I have to see if I can get him unplugged. His urethra is very small and generally it is plugged with a chalk-like material. I will try and pass a catheter and if that doesn't work, I will drain his bladder with a needle. Then after we get him empty, I must consider bladder infection and prevention in the future."

Knowing Mrs. Andre from the past, her next question was inevitable. Like I was holding a gun to her heart, she trembled and asked me, "How much is this gonna cost?"

"At this point I can't tell you. You have been here many times and you know about how our fees run. Matter of fact, last week when you were in here you commented, "I was cheaper than the other vets in town." She made no more comments about money. At the time I wondered about her remark about my cheap fees. Did she come to bury or praise me?

"How long will he have to be in the hospital?"

Tired and irritated with my impatient client and very concerned about her sick tomcat, I answered, "I don't know, just tell me what you want me to do."

"Can I use your phone to call my husband and tell him what is wrong?" I pointed to my office telephone. She grabbed it like it was a snake and started to dial the number.

I was interrupted by the sound of the front door opening. Looking up I saw Mr. Andre himself in the waiting room. He explained later when he got home from work his son told him about the cat and he rushed right over to see what was wrong.

I walked back to my office and said, "Never mind calling, he just walked in."

Once more I go through the story and tell the lady's husband what is wrong with the cat. Each minute's delay is making it harder on Tom. Poor guy, he is drooling and crying. I can smell the urine odor on his breath. He is very sick.

Mr. Andre eases the tension and said, "Sure, put him in here, Doc, he's been with us a long time. Do what you can. How much?" I interrupted him before he could finish and told him I didn't know what the final dollar amount would be. It is now five-twenty five. The clinic staff is waiting to see who has to stay and help.

Decisions made, I said, "Earl, take him back and put him on the surgery room table."

Earl is the hospital manager and has been associated with the clinic for eighteen years. He knew what to expect, not only from the sick cat and what we were going to do, but from the Andres themselves. I sent the office ladies home. I told the cat's owners I would call later in the evening when my work was done. The office help went smiling, the Andres followed, rumbling with skepticism.

As Teresa, one of my office workers, walked out the door she turned to me and said, "Doc, don't forget your six o'clock appointment."

Earl had the cat on the surgery room table, laying on his side, all claws dangerously extended, slobbering and crying in his pain and sickness.

"This one's sure sick. Do you think we dare give him an anesthetic?"

"It's risky but if we are going to save him, we have to try." Earl was standing on the scales holding the squirming cat and trying to calculate his weight. Handing the cat to me, and without getting off of the scales, mentally subtracted his own weight from the total. I asked, "How much?"

"Eleven pounds. He's damned big!"

I agreed as I filled my syringe with some Ketamine laced with a tranquilizer. This would put him to sleep and let us do our work.

The telephone rang again. Hart, who had not yet gone home, looked at me and asked, "Do you want me to answer it?" I shook my head for a negative answer.

Waiting for the anesthetic to work and the cat to relax, Earl turned on the ultrasonic unit and attached the long probe we used on a blocked urethra. Tom is now quiet, sleeping and oblivious to his suffering. Earl also hooks up the cardiac monitor and I heard the "beep, beep" it played, assuring me his pulse rate was OK I lubricate the end of the probe and attempt to insert it into the end of the cat's penis. The first attempt failed. Cats are small anatomically and the external sex organs are hard to grasp and manipulate. I glance at the clock and note it is exactly six o'clock. Finally I succeed and the probe is inserted. I step on the foot switch and activate the flow of water bubbles that are charged with the high frequency sound waves generated by the machine. At the same time, very gently so as not to bruise the tissue, I push the probe through the now open pathway into the bladder. Keeping the machine activated with the foot pedal, I slowly withdraw the probe and dressings—cat urine sprays all over the table—and me! I am soaked, face, hands, shirt and all!

A word about cat urine. In veterinary medicine there are very many odors. There is the odor of blood. In college they taught us it had no odor. They were wrong. To me, it smells. Fecal matter always has a bad odor, solid or loose. Things such as rotting tissue, vomit and others too numerous to think of, also have repulsive smells. Over the years I became accustomed to most of them but never to the odor of cat urine. For some reason I can smell cat urine if a tomcat sprays in a neighbor's yard way down the street from the clinic! If I am the first person to arrive at the clinic in the morning I go directly to the cat ward and turn on the ventilating fans and open the screened window, even if it is snowing outside! I just don't like the smell of cat urine.

Now back to Tom. He is sound asleep on my operating room table. That awful odor of urine is absolutely rank, but now since I emptied Tom's bladder, it is absolutely the best odor I ever smelled! The procedure has been a success and the old scared, thick-cheeked cat is going to be OK.

Hart is still there engrossed in what Earl and I had been doing. I asked her to call my wife and explain why I was late. She did and informed me there was another phone call that needed a reply. I took the number and after sending Hart home, I dialed it. It was Tim. He had a sick bird dog. I told him to bring it to the office—I would wait for him.

Andre's cat was now out of trouble and Earl put him in a cage. He would be OK and at this time need nothing more. I called Andre's to report and got no answer. I tried again a few minutes later and still got no answer. I gave up. Early the next morning she called and inquired if her cat had survived. "Of course," with a little sarcasm I added, "What did you expect?" I also told her I had tried to call after I finished fixing Tom but got no answer. She told me they had gone out for the evening—matter of fact, to the mall!

Three days after admittance, Tom (cat) Andre was sent home with strict instructions, medicine and a case of special cat food we routinely used in these situations. The owner wrote me a check for services. Old Tom meowed and once more climbed up her shirt. She thanked me and all was back to normal again.

Tim's dog problem was not the emergency the cat had been but it did require attention. When Tim came home from work he went to feed his dogs and one dog had some blood coming from her ear. One look convinced him she was in trouble and he agreed when his father, Terry, said, "Doctor Martin should look at her." Tim tried to call the office, got no answer so he called my house. Mary Helen told him I was still at the office and she would call on a private phone line and tell me to wait for them.

I examined the ears, and after treating them, dispensed some medicine and instructions. It was a simple outer-ear infection and the blood had come from where the old dog rubbed her head against the chain-link fence of the kennel. Origin of the infection was unknown. Prognosis for recovery was good.

Terry Mulvaney owns a plumbing company and while we were talking I asked him to replace a set of faucets on one of my sinks and replace some washers in a shut-off valve. "Doc, I appreciate you waiting on us with this dog. First of the week Tim and I will come fix it." Tim and his father went out the door, Earl and I followed. We finally called it a day.

I glanced at my watch and realized I was late for my six o'clock appointment but that was all right—it was with my wife for supper!

§   §   §

In the later years of my practice I often heard the younger doctors talk about a condition they called "burn out." I never knew what that meant and accepted the long days and the trying times as part of every day's adventures. But the older I got the more I realized there was such a problem. I found myself short-tempered and at times losing some of my compassion, not for the animals, but for the human client. Then I realized some of the old faithful weren't coming in anymore and I took time to appraise myself and my feelings. My family had been my backbone through thick and thin, good times and bad ones. I discussed it with them and after more than thirty-seven years I was tired, indeed burned out, and decided some changes had to be made for the future.

THE EGRESS

PHINEAS T. BARNUM, EARLY AMERICA'S GREATEST SHOWMAN, HOODWINKED his museum visitors with a sign over a door that said, "To The Egress." The word "egress," according to Webster's dictionary, means to "go out." The crowd, eager to see another of Barnum's wonders, crowded through the door only to find they were now outside. Their visit was over!

Like Barnum, I added some show to my practice but I worked hard at it, trying my best to serve the community, satisfy my clients and to boost my own ego. I remembered the old saying, "The wheel that squeaks the loudest, gets all the grease." I greased that wheel every chance I got and never missed a chance to boost my image and the clinic's too! Of course the familiar signs at the horse shows stating, "Jomar Farm, Division of The Martin Veterinary Clinic" was my ethical advertising and was the very best publicity a horse doctor could have.

As time went on, my own stable of horses included Lynn Genius, my good five-gaited mare, by now matriarch of the stable, Country Boy, a three-gaited champion pony that Terri showed; and my own three-gaited horse we called Bewitched. We also had a fine harness horse named Paris Lady and a new five-gaited mare we raised here on the farm. Her name was Summer Song. John Ringling North, of Ringling Brothers Barnum & Bailey Circus fame, gave Mary Helen an American quarter horse stallion from the King Ranch in Texas. His name was Royal. To keep him company, we bought a golden palomino quarter mare named Jean Holly. Of course grand master of the stable was the now retired Clinic Orderly. My horse fortune, if you want to call it that, had come a long way since the first time I ever asked my daddy for a pony!

Daughter Terri was an excellent horse person, an exceptionally good rider and was blessed with compassion and love for her animals. With my long-standing back injury, I depended on her horse interest and her riding ability to manage our show stable. She was now eighteen years old. Then one day she told her mother and me that she was going to get married. We had no trouble with this because her husband to be was Jim Klaiber, the son of John Klaiber, on whose farm years before the cow fell on me and broke my foot. They got married and moved away. I was without a rider.

In a matter of a year or so, after Terri's marriage, the show stable was disbanded and all that were left were two brood mares, the quarter horse stallion Royal, a new pony we called November, some retired circus horses and of course the aging Clinic Orderly.

These gracious animals spent their remaining days enjoying the lush bluegrass pastures at Jomar. One by one they passed on. The barns were empty, now housing only memories. Royal, The Clinic Orderly and November are buried at Jomar as are four circus horses and a circus pony that lived out their retired lives here.

Royal died on a bitter cold winter day when I was out of town. Unlike the smarter mules, my fancy quarter horse stallion gorged himself on ice-cold water which gave him a lethal case of colic. When I got back from my trip, we hired a man with a backhoe to bury him. The horse was frozen stiff and the backhoe man had to dig a very deep hole. When he was finished he gently shoved the horse into his grave. Royal landed on his feet, facing Texas! Most Texans think their state is Heaven and I guess if a horse goes to Heaven, Royal was at least pointed in that direction!

These had been grand years filled with the satisfaction of living in a beautiful part of America, the hill country of eastern Kentucky. I cherish my Kentucky experiences and the friends that I made. I saw our land evolve from rough, rural hill country without roads, electricity or telephones, bathed with many superstitions, short on formal education and long on local self-serving politics. It is not all corrected but the changes have been remarkable and now we live in a modern progressive part of the commonwealth.

Over my long career, which I cherished as a veterinarian, most of the cases, routine or unusual, turned out well. A few animals died, but generally I won the medical battles. In the long run my community and I both were the winners.

Over these many years I have often been asked, "Doctor, what is your favorite animal?"

My stock answer is always the same, "I love 'em all." And then I remember the milk wagon horse and the high stepping circus horses and my own stable of fine creatures, and I realize my true animal love is the horse. After all, that was the critter that started it all.

And now, after thirty-eight years of a rewarding career, I am retired. I didn't quit but, like Barnum's patrons, I looked for something new to see and do. So I followed the sign, "To The Egress." I went through the door to another world.